Very Interesting . . . But Stupid!
(spoken with a German accent, of course,)
was Arte Johnson's catchphrase in Rowan
and Martin's Laugh-In. It also describes the
contents of this book!

Nigel Rees has assembled an all-
embracing collection of some five hundred
show business catchphrases, many of which
have passed into the language, ranging
from those which originated in music-hall
to those still on the lips of the radio and
television stars of today. He has spoken to
many entertainers, old and young,
remembered and forgotten, to find out how
their catchphrases began, why they caught
on and why in some cases they didn't.

Anyone who has derived pleasure from
popular entertainers on radio and television
or in films, variety and music-hall will find
in this enormously enjoyable and nostalgic
book some clues as to why catchphrases
exert such a strong hold over people.

Nigel Rees's fascination with words
has already resulted in two best-selling
books, *'Quote . . . Unquote'* and *Graffiti
Lives, OK*. Thanks to a lively and varied
radio and television career and to his quiz
games 'Quote . . . Unquote' and 'Cabbages
and Kings' he has been able to pick up some
unusual snippets of show business lore.

Very Interesting . . . But Stupid! will
jog memories, recall past enjoyments and
provide fascinating footnotes to a part of
show business history.

Also by Nigel Rees in Unwin Paperbacks
'Quote . . . Unquote'
Graffiti Lives, OK
Graffiti 2
Published in hardback by
George Allen & Unwin
The 'Quote . . . Unquote' Book of Love,
Death and the Universe

A book
of catchphrases
from the world of
entertainment compiled
and introduced by
Nigel Rees

London

UNWIN PAPERBACKS

Boston   Sydney

First published in Unwin Paperbacks in 1980

UNWIN ® PAPERBACKS
40 Museum Street, London WC1A 1LU

© Nigel Rees Productions Ltd, 1980

British Library Cataloguing in Publication Data

Very interesting - but stupid!
  1. English language - Terms and phrases
  2. Entertainers - Language
I. Rees, Nigel
423'.1   PE1689

ISBN 0-04-827021-0

Art Director David Pocknell
Design Michael Cavers

Printed in Great Britain
by Cox & Wyman Limited
Reading

Acknowledgements   As I mention in the Preface, show business history largely remains unwritten -except in the form of often haphazardly compiled memoirs, sometimes little better than fan-fodder - so this makes any attempt at compiling a reference work doubly difficult. There is little to build on.

However, I am grateful to a large number of people who have helped me in my inquiries, including: Edwin Apps and Pauline Devaney; Arthur Askey; George Bartram; Bernard Bresslaw; James Casey; Charlie Chester; Gerry Collins of Manchester's Music Hall Association; Colin Crompton; Barry Cryer; Paul Daniels; Ken Dodd; Barry Day; Arthur English; Ken Goodwin; Terry Hall; Cliff Michelmore; Bob Monkhouse; Nat Mills; Frank Muir; Roger Musgrave; Jon Pertwee; Sandy Powell; Beryl Reid; Ed Stewart; Edward Taylor; Barry Took; Norman Vaughan. The staff of *Time* magazine's London Bureau and the BBC's central library in The Langham, London, were also most helpful. The BBC and Granada Television afforded me many opportunities to hear and view archive materials while working on my programmes, *'Quote . . . Unquote'* and *Cabbages And Kings*. The following books, some of which I have quoted, were useful memory-joggers:

Askey, Arthur *Before Your Very Eyes* (Woburn Press, 1975)

Barker, Eric *Steady Barker* (Secker & Warburg, 1956)

Black, Peter *The Biggest Aspidistra In The World* (BBC, 1972)

Bridgmont, Leslie *Leslie Bridgmont Presents* (Falcon Press, 1949)

Brough, Peter *Educating Archie* (Stanley Paul, 1955)

Bygraves, Max *I Wanna Tell You A Story* (W H Allen, 1976)

Campbell, Commander *When I Was In Patagonia* (Christopher Johnson, 1953)

Chester, Charlie *The World Is Full Of Charlies* (New English Library, 1974)

Clark, Kenneth *The Other Half* (John Murray, 1977)

Edwards, Jimmy *Take It From Me* (Werner Laurie, 1953)

Fisher, John *No Way To Be A Hero* (Muller, 1973)

Fletcher, Cyril *Nice One, Cyril* (Barrie & Jenkins, 1978)

Hall, Henry *Here's To The Next Time* (Odhams, 1956)

Halliwell, Leslie *Halliwell's Teleguide* (Granada 1979)

Howerd, Frankie *On The Way I Lost It* (W H Allen, 1976)

Kavanagh, Ted *The ITMA Years* (Woburn Press, 1974)

Kavanagh, Ted *Tommy Handley* (Hodder & Stoughton, 1949)

Maxwell, John *The Greatest Billy Cotton Band Show* (Jupiter, 1976)

Midwinter, Eric *Make 'Em Laugh* (George Allen & Unwin, 1979)

Milligan, Spike *More Goon Show Scripts* (Woburn Press, 1973)

Parker, Derek *Radio: The Great Years* (David & Charles, 1977)

Partridge, Eric *A Dictionary of Catch Phrases* (Routledge & Kegan Paul, 1977)

Pickles, Wilfred *Wilfred Pickles Invites You To Have Another Go* (David & Charles, 1978)

Randall, Alan and Seaton, Ray *George Formy* (W H Allen, 1974)

Ray, Ted *Raising The Laughs* (Werner Laurie, 1952)

Took, Barry *Laughter In The Air* (Robson/BBC, 1976)

Took, Barry and Feldman, Marty *Round The Horne* (Woburn Press, 1974)

Took, Barry and Feldman, Marty *The Bona Book of Julian And Sandy* (Robson, 1976)

Train, Jack *Up And Down The Line* (Odhams, 1956)

Warner, Jack *Jack Of All Trades* (W H Allen, 1975)

Worsley, Francis *ITMA 1939-1948* (Vox Mundi, 1948)

To the authors and publishers of these books my thanks are due.

Picture Acknowledgements

BBC for photographs on pages 3, 13, 15, 19, 22, 27, 29, 37, 41, 52, 67, 74, 77, 81, 92, 95, 99, 101, 106, 109, 112, 113, 115, 119, 128, 131, 133, 135, 139, 146, 149, 151, 153.

Camera Press for photographs on pages 63, 87, 110, 122, 127, 141, 157.

Keystone for photographs on pages 35, 43, 45, 57, 83, 84, 85, 104, 124, 126.

Popper photo for photograph on page 117.

Yorkshire TV for photograph on page 89.

Cover: Arte Johnson BBC photograph
Manuel BBC photograph by John Green

Preface

In the broadest sense of the word, a catchphrase is simply a phrase that has caught on. In the showbusiness sense, it is a phrase which helps identify a particular performer or show and which the audience takes up and uses until it becomes, however briefly, a part of the language.

At their worst, catchphrases can be mechanical. The temptation is for the aspiring comedian to kit himself out with a catchphrase and din it into his audience. From then on he can be sure of a round of applause whenever he utters it (an affectionate, if sheeplike, show of recognition between performer and public); he will probably record a song incorporating it; have a film or TV programme named after it; and, if he lasts long enough, he can use it as the title of his autobiography.

At their best, catchphrases live on, evocative of an era and of past pleasures, enriching the language. You will find here a catalogue of some 500 catchphrases drawn mostly from British showbusiness - some you know, some you have forgotten, and some you never knew existed! The bulk comes from radio and TV, there is a sprinkling from music-hall, variety and the cinema, and one or two from advertising. Literary catchphrases have been included only where they have been popularised through the media.

How certain catchphrases have evolved and why they exert a peculiar hold over people is in itself an interesting phenomenon . . . even if it is faintly stupid! It was not until the rise of the mass media that the catchphrase became a staple part of showbusiness. True, in the heyday of the music-hall at the turn of the century certain performers were noted for their little phrases: Marie Lloyd's **a little of what you fancy does you good!** was a line from one of her songs; **Meredith we're in!** occurred in a much-performed sketch of Fred Kitchen's. Going back even further, it appears that Shakespeare was familiar with the phenomenon. In the first quarto of *Hamlet* we read:

> You have some again, that keepes one suit of jests, as a man is known by one suit of apparel, and gentlemen quote his jests down in their tables before they come to the play, as thus: Cannot you stay till I eat my porridge? and, You owe a quarter's wages; and, Your beer is sour.

Not until the 1930s, however, and the arrival of the kind of radio comedy which evolved from *Band Waggon* were conditions ripe for catchphrases to become commonplace. Shows like *Band Waggon* and *ITMA* had two key ingredients: regularity and feedback. Catchphrases could be used every week (whereas a music-hall performer doing his rounds might be seen in one place at most a couple of times a year) and the studio audiences helped them catch on by their infectiously enthusiastic response which spread to listeners at home. Because repetition is lacking, comparatively few phrases have come out of the cinema.

The heyday of the catchphrase was undoubtedly when British radio was at its peak - from about 1939 to the introduction of commercial TV in 1955. During its ten-year run, straddling the war, *ITMA* made use of approximately fifty catchphrases. Indeed, at times, the show appeared to contain little else. There would be a knock at the famous *ITMA* door, the character would engage in a little banter with Tommy

Handley, the catchphrase would be delivered (often receiving a giant ovation), and then the next one would be wheeled in. It is not easy now to appreciate why the show was so popular. But the laughter undoubtedly took people's minds off the war and the programmes brought together the whole country, fostering a family feeling and sense of sharing which in itself encouraged the spread of catchphrases. The writing is not to everyone's taste now (it relied heavily on feeble puns) but Tommy Handley's brisk, cheerful personality was the magic ingredient which held the proceedings together.

The scripting of later radio comedy shows, such as *Take It From Here* and *The Goon Show,* was vastly superior, but they still made liberal use of catchphrases. *TIFH* generated about half a dozen; the Goons took quite a few from music-hall as well as launching their own brand, producing a total score of about twenty-five.

Other leaders in the catchphrase stakes over the years have been *Ray's A Laugh* (about eighteen) and *Educating Archie* (seventeen) and various shows associated with Kenneth Horne (seventeen) and Arthur Askey (fifteen).

When TV became the main form of entertainment, a certain reaction against the catchphrase seems to have set in. Individual performers such as Tommy Cooper and Charlie Drake launched their own. Bruce Forsyth has had about five and Morecambe and Wise ten. And a good number came out of situation comedies, ranging from *The Army Game* to *Are You Being Served?* But TV comedy now largely manages without catchphrases and the new breed of university-graduate comedians often eschews them altogether, out of a feeling that they belong to an alien showbiz world (though *Monty Python* gave rise to one or two).

The big exception to this trend was *Rowan And Martin's Laugh-In* imported from the United States in the late 1960s. *Laugh-In* had at least sixteen catchphrases, ranging from **sock it to me!** to the one used as the title of this book. But other attempts to revive the quickfire formula have generally failed. Perhaps most people prefer comedy based on character and situation.

I have included one or two catchphrases which started life in TV commercials because this form of advertising strikes me as a branch of entertainment. Here we are faced with the distinction between phrases which have genuinely caught on and phrases which have been deliberately planted or have become familiar through frequent repetition. I have not been very strict in policing this demarcation line. Also, I have included some stock phrases from radio or TV which are not catchphrases in the strict sense of the word, some verbal tics - the sort of mannerisms impressionists seize on -and (for interest's sake) a number of failed catchphrases.

True catchphrases - ones that have entered the language - are by and large those which can be employed pretty regularly in day-to-day situations. The classics from *ITMA* **(can I do you now, sir?/ I don't mind if I do!/ after you, Claude - no, after you, Cecil!)** have lasted over twenty years because they can be used to cover social embarrassment, whether performing a service, accepting the offer of a drink, or going through a doorway. The shared knowledge implied somehow lessens the embarrassment, obscures the difficulty.

This quality of sharing an 'in' thing

lies at the heart of the use of catchphrases in ordinary conversation. They become verbal lubricants, if you like; an exchange of recognition tokens. People also like a little mindless repetition. A former TV critic recalls how his wife and he still say to each other **'your hands are grimy'** / **'grimy? oh, blimey!'** even though it is forty years since they first heard the phrase on *ITMA* and almost everybody else has forgotten it.

Many of the best catchphrases come about by accident. They suddenly emerge, get seized on by the audience, and catch on. But quite a few have been deliberately and successfully concocted. Bob Monkhouse avers that a gilt-edged catchphrase should be 'perfectly in character, arise naturally, be short, funny in any setting, and *useful*'; yet he admits that **Bernie, the bolt!** was carefully engineered like an industrial product!

One should say that a lot of these phrases were in use long before they became associated with a particular performer. Where an entertainer's name is mentioned it is because he popularised the words and made them, to an extent, his own.

A book of catchphrases is, in a manner of speaking, a series of footnotes to show business history - a history which is, by the way, largely unwritten. My own memories of the pleasures of entertainment only go back to about 1951, when I was seven. So I have had to rely on a number of sources to help me in the more archaeological parts of my quest. There are bound to be omissions and mistakes and I would be delighted to be told about them. A full list of acknowledgements can be found on pages 5-6.

No book dealing with this by-way of language could fail to make mention of the late Eric Partridge. I never had any dealings with him but his *Dictionary of Catch Phrases,* although a product of his later years and taking a much broader view of the subject than this book, encouraged me to proceed.

So, *that's the way it is, folks!*

I shall *say no more!*

and *orft we jolly well go then!*

after you Claude - no, after you, Cecil! One
of the most enduring *ITMA* catchphrases.
Spoken originally by Horace Percival and
Jack Train playing two over-polite
handymen, Cecil and Claude respectively, it
still survives as an admirable way of
overcoming social awkwardness in such
matters as who should go through a door
first. (*ITMA* was first broadcast on 12 July
1939 and ran until January 1949, when
Tommy Handley died.)

ain't it a shame, eh? ain't it a shame?
Another *ITMA* phrase, spoken by Carleton
Hobbs as the nameless man who told banal
tales ('I waited for hours in the fish queue
. . . and a man took my plaice') and always
prefaced and concluded them with 'aint it a
shame?'

all human life is there! A *News of the
World* advertising slogan which took on a
certain life of its own in the rest of the
world. (See also **nice one, Cyril!**).

all right! Verbal tic of Alan 'Fluff'
Freeman, the DJ.

all we want is the facts, ma'am! Jack Webb
as Joe Friday, the fast-talking cop in the
American TV series *Dragnet* (1951-8,
1967-9).

always merry and bright! Alfred Lester,
music-hall star - who was always
lugubrious, needless to say.

**and now for something completely
different!** From the BBC TV series *Monty
Python's Flying Circus,* first broadcast in
1969. When I used to introduce Radio 4's
breakfast-time *Today* programme I often
found cause to regret that the Python team

had turned this into a catchphrase. After all, if you are introducing a certain type of magazine programme there's not much else you can say to link an interview with the Prime Minister to an item about beer-drinking cows! The phrase was also used as the title of Monty Python's first feature film.

and the best of luck! Frankie Howerd claims to have given this phrase immortality: 'It came about when I introduced into radio *Variety Bandbox* those appallingly badly sung mock operas, starring the show's bandleader Billy Ternent (tenor), Madame Vere-Roper (soprano) and Frankie Howerd (bass - "the lowest of the low"). Vera while singing would pause for breath before a high C and as she mustered herself for this musical Everest I would mutter, "And the best of luck!" Later it became: "And the best of British luck!" The phrase is so common now that I frequently surprise people when I tell them it was my catchphrase on *Variety Bandbox.'*

Eric Partridge suggests, however, that the longer version was originally a Second World War army phrase ironically meaning the exact opposite of what it appeared to, and compares it with a line from the First World War song:

> Over the top with the best of luck
> Parley-voo.

and the next object . . . ! Phrase used by the Mystery Voice in the radio quiz *Twenty Questions* - raised to catchphrase level by Norman Hackforth's deep, fruity rendering of such gems as: 'And the next object is . . . the odour in the larder.'

and the next 'Tonight' is tomorrow night, good night! Stock concluding phrase of the original BBC TV *Tonight* programme, 1957-65. Cliff Michelmore, who used to say it, comments: 'The combined brains of Alasdair Milne, Donald Baverstock, myself and three others were employed to come up with the phrase. There were at least ten others tried and permed. At least we cared . . . !'

and there's more where that came from!
Sometimes said by Major Bloodnok (Peter
Sellers) and occasionally by Wallace
Greenslade, the announcer, in the highly
esteemed *Goon Show*. (The Goons -Sellers,
Harry Secombe and Spike Milligan - first
appeared in a radio show called *Crazy
People* on 28 May 1951. They lasted until
January 1960, with one extra programme in
1972.)

and with that, I return you to the studio!
The standard outside broadcast
commentator or reporter's line, given new
life when used by Cecil Snaith (Hugh
Paddick), the hush-voiced BBC man in
Beyond Our Ken. Used, as a rule, after
describing some disaster in which he had
figured. Kenneth Horne suggested the line.

Anthea, give us a twirl! Bruce Forsyth to
hostess Anthea Redfern in BBC TV's
Generation Game (inviting her to show off
her dress, perhaps I should add).

'appen? Robin Bailey as Uncle Mort, the
scuffling, seedy old mysogynist in Peter
Tinniswood's TV series *I Didn't Know You
Cared*.

aren't plums cheap? The catchphrase of
comedy acrobat/contortionist, Bob Nelson,
'The Naval Comic'. He would entangle
himself in a number of balancing bentwood
chairs and made the remark to hold the
audience's interest while he had another go
at disentangling himself.

are yer courtin'? One of the questions
Wilfred Pickles would use nudgingly in his
long-running radio quiz *Have A Go,*
chatting up spinster contestants of any age
from nineteen to ninety.

are you going to pardon me? Mr Muggs (Charles Hawtrey) in *Ray's A Laugh*. (Ted Ray's radio programme, rich in catchphrases, was first broadcast on 4 April 1949 and ran until 1960.)

are you married? Hetty, the amorous character played by Dick Emery.

(hey) are you putting it round that I'm barmy? The splendidly named Hutton Conyers, to Jimmy James.

are you sitting comfortably? (Then I'll begin) The customary way of beginning a story on radio's *Listen With Mother* since about 1950. Julia Lang is credited with introducing the phrase.

arriverderci! Willie Joss in a Scottish radio show *It's All Yours, circa* 1952.

'as 'e bin' in, whack? Question repeatedly put to Dave Morris, the manager of radio's *Club Night* in the 1950s. 'E never 'ad, of course.

as if I cared! Sam Fairfechan (played by Hugh Morton) in *ITMA*. He would say, 'Good morning, how are you today?' and immediately follow with 'As if I cared.' The character derived his name from Llanfairfechan, the seaside resort in North Wales where Ted Kavanagh, *ITMA's* scriptwriter, resided when the BBC Variety Department was evacuated to nearby Bangor during the early part of the Second World War.

as it happens! Jimmy Savile OBE's verbal tic, which is an identifying mark if not actually a catchphrase. He used it as the title of his autobiography but when the book came out in paperback this was changed to *Love Is An Uphill Thing* because (or so it was suggested) the word 'love' in a title ensured more sales.

as the art mistress said to the gardener! A variation of the traditional double-entendre mechanism 'as the Bishop said to the actress', this originated during Beryl Reid's stint as Monica in *Educating Archie*. (I have always used it in preference to the original.)

aye, aye, that's yer lot! Jimmy Wheeler (1910-73) was a cockney comedian with a fruity voice redolent of beer, jellied eels and winkles. He would appear in a bookmaker's suit, complete with spiv moustache and hat, and play the violin. At the end of his fiddle piece he would break off his act and intone this catchphrase.

ay thang yew! Arthur Askey's distinctive pronunciation of his catchphrase, 'I thank you!' He says he picked it up from the cry of London bus conductors. First used by him in *Band Waggon*. Later, the title of a film. 'I didn't know I was saying it till people used to shout it at me!' Arthur recalls.

back to square one! This expression meaning 'back to the very beginning' gained currency in the 1930s because of its use by radio football commentators. *Radio Times* used to print a 'map' of the football field divided into numbered squares, to which commentators would refer. Obviously, however, there is an echo of Snakes and Ladders about the phrase.

banjaxed! Word used by Terry Wogan. Of obscure origin and, indeed, meaning.

beautiful downtown Burbank! Rowan and Martin in their *Laugh-In* coined this ironic compliment to the place in Los Angeles where NBC TV studios are situated. A quintessential late 1960s sound was that of the announcer, Gary Owens, intoning 'This is beautiful downtown Burbank.' *Laugh-In* was broadcast from 1967-72 and briefly revived in 1977.

(here and now) before your very eyes! In the early 1950s Arthur Askey was discussing with the BBC's Ronnie Waldman an idea for his first TV series. He registered the title *Before Your Very Eyes* there and then, before he had even got the series, because of its obvious appropriateness.

Bernie, the bolt! Bob Monkhouse, once compère of ATV's long-running quiz *The Golden Shot,* explains: 'I dislike the notion of a conscientiously created catchphrase. The best, it appears to me, have been borne spontaneously and survived because of their multiple applications. "Bernie, the bolt!" broke all my own rules.

'Lew Grade, now Lord Grade, had bought the Swiss-German TV success, *The Golden Shot.* The first host, Jackie Rae, had to repeat one line eight times in each show -the word of instruction to the technician to load the dangerous crossbows and simultaneously warn the studio of the fact that the weapon was armed - "Heinz, the bolt!"

'When I took over in 1967 I increased the number of times he would have to load the crossbows from eight to fifteen. But a lucky chance saved me from finding 57 ways of saying Heinz. Heinz went home. He stayed long enough to train an ATV technician, Derek Young. "Grand," I said. "Derek, the bolt - that sounds lousy. Let's make it alliterative. What's funny and begins with B?" Colin Clews, the producer, favoured Basil. I liked Bartholomew. We were reckoning without the man himself. Derek liked Derek.

' "Well, *you* think of a name that begins with B and won't embarrass you," I said. And Bernie it became. I found out later that his wife liked it. Certainly the audience did. Only blokes called Bernie grew to loathe it. From the start, the catchphrase that broke my rules - lacking spontaneous birth, character, alternative applications, and so patently constructed for the purpose - became a part of British TV folklore. Thousands of letters were addressed simply to "Bernie the Bolt, ITV."

'When the now successful series was moved
from ATV's Borehamwood studios to
Birmingham for what was to be a further
seven years, fifty-two Sundays per year, it
meant that Derek Young had to train a
Midlands-based technician. "What name
are you going to call the armourer now?"
he asked. "Well, Bernie, of course. We
can't change the catchphrase." "But *I'm*
Bernie, the Bolt." He suddenly gave in with
a shrug and said, "Well, that's showbiz."

'I spoke the magic three little words for
the last time on 13 April 1975. At a
conservative estimate, I said them on
network TV no less than 2,500 times. On a
May night in 1979 I found written in the
dust on my car outside a Nottingham
cabaret club:"BERNIE THE BOLT
LIVES!" '

Beulah, peel me a grape! A phrase of
dismissive unconcern, first uttered by Mae
West to a black maid in the film *I'm No
Angel* (1933) after a male admirer had
stormed out on her.

BFN - 'bye for now! A common
catchphrase even before Jimmy Young
adopted it as a way of signing off his disc-
and-chat shows on Radios 1 and 2. Perhaps
it links back to *ITMA's* 'TTFN!'

Big Brother is watching you! This is one of
the few catchphrases to have arisen from a
novel - George Orwell's *1984*. The spectre
of an all-seeing authority somehow
contriving to spy on every member of
society put the phrase into the language
soon after the book's publication in 1949.
The sensational impact of the BBC's TV

adaptation in 1954 further popularised the phrase and it was well established by the time of the government surveillance scandals of the 1960s and '70s.

big 'ead! A moment from *Educating Archie* in 1956:
Ken Platt: I suppose you don't know this fellow coming in with the big head?
Archie Andrews: Big head? Yes, of course I know him. Hello, Mr Bygraves.
Max Bygraves ran into a little trouble with educationalists who thought he ought to pronounce the 'h' in 'big head' but he persisted with a song ('Why does everybody call me "Big 'ead"?') and with an act which lasts to this day, cleverly based on a form of mock conceit.

big-hearted Arthur (that's me)! 'I have always used this expression,' says Arthur Askey, 'even when I was at school. When playing cricket, you know, if the ball was hit to the boundary and nobody would go and fetch it, I would, saying "Big-hearted Arthur, that's me!" ' It was included in the first edition of *Band Waggon* - which was really the first radio comedy show (as opposed to one made up of variety acts) -on 5 January 1938.
'There had been radio comedians before this who used catchphrases, like Sandy Powell, but ours was the first show which really made a thing of them,' says Arthur. 'I was the one who was on the air most and kept banging them in.'
To that extent, Arthur may be said to have originated the use of catchphrases in a big way on radio. The basic format of *Band Waggon* was that of a magazine but the best remembered segment is Arthur sharing

a flat with Richard Murdoch at the top of Broadcasting House as 'resident comedians.'

black mark, Bentley! Jimmy Edwards in radio's *Take It From Here* (referring to Dick Bentley). Frank Muir, who wrote the scripts for *TIFH* with Denis Norden, says the phrase arose from the use of 'black mark' by James Robertson Justice in Peter Ustinov's film of *Vice-Versa*. (*TIFH* was first broadcast on 23 March 1948).

blue pencil! Jack Warner in radio's *Garrison Theatre* (first broadcast 6 January 1940) can claim a good deal of credit for introducing 'blue pencil' as a synonym for 'censor'. Recitations out of blue-pencilled letters from his 'brother' at the Front led to expletives being deleted ('not blue pencil likely!') and to Warner's mother boasting that 'My John, with his blue pencil gag, has stopped the whole nation from swearing'. In his autobiography, Warner recalls a constable giving evidence at a London police court about stopping 'Mr Warner, a lorry driver'. The magistrate inquired, 'Did he ask what the blue pencil you wanted?' 'No, sir,' replied the constable, 'this was a different Mr Warner . . .''

boom, boom! Verbal underlining to the punch-line of a gag. Ernie Wise suggests that it is like the drum thud or trumpet sting used, particularly by Americans, to point a joke. Music-hall star Billy Bennett (who died in 1942) may have been the first to use this device to emphasise his comic couplets. Morecambe and Wise, Basil Brush and many others have taken it up.

boy wonder! Batman's commendation of his hench person, Robin. (*The Burkiss Way's* alternative 'bay window' has rather more edge, I feel.)

brand-y-y-y-y'! Accompanied by the sound of retreating running footsteps, *The Goon Show's* beloved way of getting anybody out of a situation that was too much for them.

brill! Little and Large.

bumper bundle! 'At home and away it's time for *Family Favourites'*; the sweeping strings of the signature tune 'With A Song In My Heart'; the smell of roast and gravy wafting out of the kitchen - a potent memory of Sunday mornings in the early 1950s (see also **wakey-wakey!**). Cliff Michelmore, who used to introduce the programme with Jean Metcalfe at either end of a Germany-UK link-up, says 'The phrase "bumper bundle" was invented by my wife, Jean. Her road to Damascus was at the crossroads on Banstead Heath one Sunday morning when driving in to do the programme. It was used to include a large number of requests all for the same record, especially "Top Ten" hits, *circa* 1952-3.' The programme was first broadcast as *Family Favourites* on 7 October 1945 and became *Two-Way Family Favourites* on 3 January 1960.

but I'm all right now! Sophie Tuckshop (Hattie Jacques) stuffing herself and squealing in *ITMA*.

byeee! (falsetto) Ed Stewart. (See **morning!**)

by gum, she's a hot 'un! Frank Randle, the variety star of the 1930s and '40s, used this phrase in a sketch in which he appeared as a hiker approximately eighty-two years old and obsessed with ale and girls' legs. Randle (1901-57), whose fame was restricted to the north of England, would also say **any more fer sailing'?** and **by gum, ah've supped sum ale toneet!**

by Jove, I needed that! Ken Dodd, after a 'a quick burst on the banjo' to relieve tension. Also used in *The Goon Show*.

can I do you now, sir? One of the great catchphrases of all time. Said by Mrs Mopp (Dorothy Summers), the hoarse-voiced charlady or 'Corporation Cleanser', when entering the office of Tommy Handley, the Mayor, in *ITMA*. Curiously, the first time Mrs Mopp used the phrase (on 10 October 1940) she said, 'Can I do *for* you now, sir?' This was soon replaced by the more familiar emphases, 'Can I *do* you *now, sir?'* Still to be heard today.

can you hear me, mother? 'It was 1932-3,' recalls Sandy Powell; 'I was doing an hour's show on the radio, live, from Broadcasting House in London, and doing a sketch called "Sandy at the North Pole". I was supposed to be broadcasting home and wanting to speak to my mother. When I got to the line, "Can you hear me, mother?" I dropped my script on the studio floor. While I was picking up the sheets all I could do was repeat the phrase over and over. Well, that was on a Saturday night. The following week I was appearing at the Hippodrome, Coventry, and the manager came to me at the band rehearsal with a request: "You'll say that, tonight, won't you?" I said, "What?" He said, "Can you hear me, mother? Everybody's saying it. Say it and see." So I did and the whole audience joined in and I've been stuck with it ever since. Even abroad - New Zealand, South Africa, Rhodesia, they've all heard it. I'm not saying it was the first radio catchphrase -they were all trying them out - but it was the first to catch on.'

Cardew do? Cardew Robinson. (See also **how do you do?**)

carry on, London! From just before the Second World War and for many years afterwards the BBC's *In Town Tonight* was the nearest radio came to a chat show. It was introduced by what sounds like a very quaint montage of 'Knightsbridge March' by Eric Coates, traffic noises, a violet-seller in Piccadilly Circus, and then a stentorian voice - which I always believed (wrongly) to be Lord Reith's - saying 'Stop!' Then an announcer would intone: 'Once again we stop the mighty roar of London's traffic and from the great crowds we bring you some of the interesting people who have come by land, sea and air to be "In Town Tonight".' At the end of the programme, to get the traffic moving again, the stentorian voice would bellow, 'Carry on, London!' The first person to say it was Freddie Grisewood.

carry on smokin'! Sub-Lieutenant Eric 'Heartthrob' Barker in the navy version of the radio show *Merry Go Round,* which ran from 1943 to 1948. Each of the three services took it in turns to be featured and the shows were mainly written and performed by men and women in the services. The Navy edition, which revolved around *HMS Waterlogged* eventually turned into *Waterlogged Spa;* the Army edition became *Stand Easy;* and the Air Force edition, *Much Binding in the Marsh.* Sometimes referred to as *Mediterranean Merry Go Round.*

Char-har-lie! / **'Allo, what do you want, Ingrid?** An exchange between Pat Hayes and Fred Yule in *Ray's A Laugh.*

cheeky monkey! Al Read. (See **right monkey!**)

chilly! Frankie Howerd.

clumsy clot! Jimmy Edwards in *Take It From Here* - a hangover from RAF wartime slang.

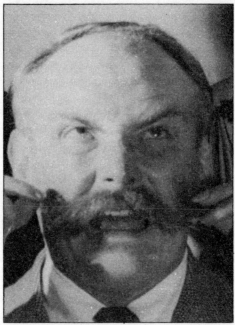

come to Charlee-ee! Chester, of course: 'I would talk to somebody from the stage and say, "Are you all right, Ada? Speak to Charlee-ee. Charlie spoke to *you*!" And I thought, what a marvellous idea for a title. So one radio show was called *A Proper Charlie* because it was based on me being an idiot and I followed it up with *Come to Charlee-ee.* You'd be surprised how many people still ask, "Say that phrase for me!" "What phrase is that?" "Say, 'come to

Charlee-ee!'" It's just one of those things they like to hear.' (See also **now there's a beaut if ever there was one!**)

come up and see me sometime! A rare example of a line from a film becoming a catchphrase. However, Mae West does not quite say these words in her 1933 picture *She Done Him Wrong*. What she does say (to a very young Cary Grant) is: 'You know I always did like a man in uniform. And that one fits you grand. Why don't you *come up some time and see me?'* The easier to-articulate version is said to Mae West by W C Fields in *My Little Chickadee* (1939).

concentrated cacophony! Deryck Guyler's archetypical scouser Frisby Dyke in *ITMA* found this a bit hard to understand. After a burst of noisy music:
Tommy Handley: Never in the whole of my three hundred *ITMA's* have I ever heard such a piece of concentrated cacophony.
Frisby Dyke: What's 'concentrated cacophony?'

coughin' well tonight! A tragically true remark about himself used by George Formby Senior, 'the Wigan Nightingale'. He had a convulsive cough which eventually killed him - the result of a tubercular condition (1921).

dabra, dabra!

dabra, dabra! (followed by stuttering) Jon Pertwee as Weatherby Wett in *Waterlogged Spa,* later becoming Commander Weatherby in *The Navy Lark,* another long-running radio series.

dad! . . . dad! Al Read.

daft as a brush! The Northern expression 'soft as a brush' adapted by Ken Platt. 'I started saying this when I was doing shows in the Army in the early 1940s,' Ken says. 'People used to write and tell me I'd got it wrong!'

damn clever these Chinese! A Second World War phrase taken up from time to time by *The Goon Show.*

the day war broke out! A catchphrase created for radio by Robb Wilton (1881-1957). 'The day war broke out, my missus looked at me and said, "Eh! What good are you?" ' When circumstances changed, amended to 'the day *peace* broke out'.

desist! One of a number of mock-disapproving phrases employed by George Robey, 'the Darling of the Halls', who died in 1954 at the age of eighty-five. 'If there is any more hilarity you must leave. Pray temper your hilarity with a modicum of reserve. Desist! I am surprised at you, Agnes!' (pronounced 'Ag-er-ness'). Also, 'desist, refrain and cease', 'Go *out*!', 'Get *out*!' or simply '*Out*!'

diddy! 'Diddy Uncle Jack' was how the family used to describe Ken Dodd's great-uncle. Ken now uses the word to describe anything 'quaint, small and lovable'. 'My family', he says, 'always impressed on me the importance of being original in my act and I suppose these words I use, like "diddy", "full of plumptiousness" and "tattifilarious", are an attempt at having something which is mine and nobody else's.'

did I ever tell you about the time I was in Sidi Barrani? Kenneth Horne, by way of introduction to a boring anecdote, in *Much Binding In The Marsh.*

didn't he do well? Compliment from Bruce Forsyth to contestant in *The Generation Game.* It is said to have arisen *circa* 1973 with what a studio attendant used to shout from the lighting grid during rehearsals.

discumknockerating! Another catchword of Ken Dodd, expressing that something bowls you over.

dodgy! Rather as the upper classes tend to rely on two adjectives - 'fascinating' and 'boring' - so, too, did the comedian Norman Vaughan in the 1960s. Accompanied by a downward gesture of the thumb, his 'dodgy' was the equivalent of the upper-class 'boring'. (See also **swingin'!**)

doesn't it make you want to spit! Arthur Askey admits he was rapped over the knuckles for introducing this 'unpleasant' expression on *Band Waggon.* 'Reith thought it a bit vulgar but I was in the driving seat - the show was so popular - so he couldn't fire me. I suppose I said it all the more!'

dollar lolly! Max Bygraves, during his period as Archie's tutor in *Educating Archie,* the early 1950s, when the free-spending American was particularly noticeable in post-austerity Britain.

don't be filthy! Arthur Askey in *Band Waggon.*

don't be fright! Sirdani, the radio magician (sic), *circa* 1944.

(aw) don't embarrass me! Ventriloquist Terry Hall first created Lenny the Lion from a bundle of fox-fur and papier-mâché (with a golf-ball for a nose) in 1954. He gave his new partner a gentle lisping voice, added a few mannerisms and a catchphrase which began thus: 'He's Ferocious!' (drum roll) 'He's courageous!' (drum roll) 'He's the King of the Jungle!' There was nothing to top this except for the lion to say, 'Aw, don't embarrass me!'
Unusually, given the success of the catchphrase, Terry Hall drops it from time to time, arguing that it's no bad policy to rest certain material and then resuscitate it.

don't force it, Phoebe! A Charlie Chester phrase from the post-Second World War radio show *Stand Easy.* Charlie remembers that this began as a joke in medical sketches: "The doctor said 'drop 'em', so I put my shopping bag down," you know, that sort of thing. Or there was a notice on the wall outside saying "No Talking" and one further in saying "No Smoking" and in the nurses' room it would say just "No". And I had a vision of this nurse putting a needle in the arm. She says to me, "Do you dance?" I said "No", so she says, "You will in a minute. The needle's very blunt!" And I thought - "Well . . . don't force it,

Phoebe!'' I found that it not only fitted there, it fitted everywhere else.'

don't forget the diver! One of *ITMA's* most illustrious phrases (spoken by Horace Percival as the diver). It was taken from Tommy Handley's memories of a man who used to dive off New Brighton pier on the Wirral around 1920. 'Don't forget the diver, sir, don't forget the diver,' he would say, collecting money in a fishing net. 'Every penny makes the water warmer, sir -every penny makes the water warmer.' The radio character first appeared in 1940 and no lift went down for the next few years without somebody using these repetitions or 'I'm going down now, sir!'
An eyewitness of the actual diver recalls: 'I thought him very brave. Although tough-looking, he was not so young, only had one leg, and used to dive from a great height as passengers left the ferry boat from Liverpool. He would stand poised first and call to them as they waited for the gangway to go down, ''Don't forget the diver, I rely entirely on your generosity.'' His assistant held a fishing net on a pole across from the pier to the jetty where the passengers popped in their contributions. Often he had a very small ''catch''. After diving he would climb the vertical steps to the pier ready for the next boat in. He was encased in what looked like a black rubber diving suit and helmet, and was, I think, a casualty of the First World War. Although he was made famous later by *ITMA* as a figure of fun, I never saw him smile!'

don't forget the fruit gums, mum! An advertising slogan for Rowntree's fruit gums which acquired a certain amount of usage in the language generally. Coined by copy-writer Roger Musgrave, who also devised **poor cold Fred!** for the Electricity Council. (See also **nice one, Cyril!**)

don't some mothers have 'em? An old Lancashire saying popularised by Jimmy Clitheroe in radio's *The Clitheroe Kid*, which ran from 1958 to 1972 (when the little lad died at the age of fifty-seven). Later, as *Some Mothers Do 'Ave 'Em,* the title of Michael Crawford's TV series.

don't you know there's a war on? A response to complaints, used by (Will) Hatton and (Ethel) Manners as a cockney chappie and Lancashire lass in their variety act.

down, Upsey! Joan Harben as a fast-talking character in *ITMA,* to her dog.

do you mind! A variation of 'mind your own business'. Kenneth Connor as Sidney Mincing in *Ray's A Laugh.* Appearing in a different situation each week, Mincing was usually some sort of unhelpful, down-beat shop assistant and was introduced thus:
Ted Ray (in furniture store): It looks like a contemptuous lamp-standard with a weird looking shade.
Mincing: Do you mind! My name is Sidney Mincing and I happen to be the proprietor of this dishpans, fryingpans and Peter Pans (as it's all on the Never-Never) emporium. What can I do for you!

drop the gun, Louis! Another impressionist's phrase that appears to have been invented rather than quoted. What Humphrey Bogart says to Claude Rains in *Casablanca* is no more than 'Not so fast, Louis!'

elementary, my dear Watson! Although seemingly literary in origin, the Sherlock Holmes catchphrase really came out of the film and broadcast versions of the Conan Doyle stories. Nowhere in the originals does the great detective say this phrase in so many words. However in *The Memoirs Of Sherlock Holmes* he does exclaim 'Elementary!' at one point to Dr Watson.

'ello darlin'! A young cockney lad intoned this greeting into Ed 'Stewpot' Stewart's tape-recorder when he was visiting a hospital for *Junior Choice* in about 1971. The tape has been played countless times since as a kind of verbal jingle but the identity of the speaker has never been discovered. Ed says: 'I didn't play back the tape for three or four months and in any case I hadn't made a note of the speaker's name - so I've no idea who, or where, the phrase came from.'

Emily and her twinges! In *Much Binding In The Marsh* Sam Costa would make his exit referring to this lady and her problem.

'ere mush! Occasional couth locution of one Francis Howerd, comedian.

evening all! Accompanied by a shaky salute to the helmet - who else but PC George Dixon (Jack Warner) in TV's *Dixon Of Dock Green*. (See also **mind how you go!**)

ever so! The 'Ever So' girls in *ITMA*.

everybody out! Miriam Karlin in her best flame-thrower voice, as Paddy, the cockney shop-stewardess in *The Rag Trade*. This programme had the unusual distinction of running on BBC TV from 1961 to 1965, then being revived by London Weekend

Television from 1977.

everybody wants to get into the act! Jimmy 'Schnozzle' Durante.

excuse me, is this the place? are you the bloke? A frequent Jimmy James expression.

exterminate! exterminate! The BBC's science-fiction series *Dr Who* has given rise to numerous beasties but none so successful as the Daleks - mobile pepper-pots with antennae whose metallic voices bark out 'exterminate! exterminate!' as they set about doing so with ray guns. Much imitated by children.

eyaydon, yauden, yaydon, negidicrop dibombit! Jon Pertwee as Svenson, the Norwegian stoker, in Navy *Merry Go Round,* whose cod Norwegian (based on close scrutiny of wartime news broadcasts) always ended up with these words.

(the) fickle finger of fate This was the name given to a mock talent show segment of *Laugh-In*. ('Who knows when the Fickle Finger of Fate may beckon *you* to stardom?')

(the) fight on flab Terry Wogan's name for the physical jerks he once used to encourage listeners to indulge in on his Radio 2 programme. He himself managed to lose two of the sixteen stone he weighed when he first came to Britain from Ireland (and that was off his head alone!).

(the) Fleet's lit up! The most famous broadcasting boob of all time. Lieutenant-Commander Tommy Woodrooffe was a leading BBC radio commentator of the 1930s. In May 1937 he was due to give a fifteen-minute description of the illumination of the Fleet on the night of the Spithead naval review. 'I was so overcome by the occasion', he told the *News Chronicle,* 'that I literally burst into tears ... . I found I could say no more.'
What Woodrooffe began by saying was: 'At the present moment the whole Fleet's lit up. When I say "lit up", I mean lit up by fairy lamps.' He repeated this information several times, varying the phraseology. Then he said: 'There's no Fleet. It's disappeared! I was talking to you in the middle of this damn - in the middle of this fleet - and what's happened is the Fleet's gone - disappeared and gone.'
Eventually, an announcer said: 'The broadcast from Spithead is now at an end. It is eleven minutes to eleven, and we will take you back to the broadcast from the Carlton Hotel Dance Band.'
That familiar BBC figure, A. Spokesman,

commented later: 'We regret that the commentary was unsatisfactory and for that reason it was curtailed.' Naturally many listeners concluded that Woodrooffe himself had been 'lit up' as the result of too much hospitality from his former shipmates on board HMS *Nelson*. But he denied this. 'I had a kind of nervous blackout. I had been working too hard and my mind just went blank.'

Certainly the BBC took a kindly view and the incident did not put paid to Woodrooffe's broadcasting career. In 1938 and 1939 he was the only commentator for the FA Cup Final, the Grand National and the Derby. Commentating on the Cup Final, he declared in the closing minutes: 'If there's a goal scored now I'll eat my hat.' There was, and he did. When war broke out he returned to the navy and did little broadcasting after 1939. He died in 1978.

flippin' kids! The 'catchphrase of the year' in 1951, according to Peter Brough, in whose *Educating Archie* it was spoken by Tony Hancock as yet another of the dummy's long line of tutors. For a while, 'the lad 'imself' was billed as 'Tony (Flippin' Kids) Hancock' before moving on to his own shows, which more or less eschewed the use of catchphrases.

Friday! A catchword from *ITMA*. Any remark ending with the word - or one sounding like it - would bring the response, 'Friday?' and the counter-response, 'Friday!'

funny! Peter Cook says that this caught on between himself and Dudley Moore as Pete and Dud in TV's *Not Only . . . But Also* but not with the world at large. Fozzy Bear tried in *The Muppet Show* also to make it catch on, pronouncing it 'fun-neee!'

(a) funny thing happened (to me) on the way to the theatre (tonight) . . . ! Traditional comedian's lead-in to joke. Origin not known.

gentlemen, be seated! Injunction by 'Mr Interlocutor' to black minstrels.

gently Bentley! Jimmy Edwards used to growl this euphonious coinage at Dick Bentley in *Take It From Here.*

George, don't do that! Not a proper catchphrase but a quotation from Joyce Grenfell's Nursery School sketches. Part of its charm lay in our not ever knowing *what* it was that George was doing.

get out of that! A line to go with one of what Morecambe and Wise describe as their *visual* catchphrases. Ernie Wise recalls, 'We were in a summer season at Morecambe with Alma Cogan in 1961 when it first arose. Eric put his hand under my chin like a judo hold.'
Their other visual catchphrases include: the 'throttling' of Eric, which appears to happen as he goes through the gap in a theatre-curtain but is, of course, self-inflicted; the imaginery stone which thuds into a paperbag held out to catch it; Eric's spectacles hooked over one ear and under the other; the rapid self-slap on the back of the neck; Eric's two handed-slap of Ernie's cheeks; the shoulder hug; and their characteristic dance with hands alternately behind head and bottom while they hop in deliberate emulation of Groucho Marx.

give him the money, Barney! Radio's *Have A Go* was to the 1940s and 1950s what TV's *Generation Game* was to the 1970s - a simple quiz which enabled the hosts, Wilfred Pickles and Bruce Forsyth, both accompanied by their respective wives, Mabel Pickles and Anthea Redfern, to indulge in folksy chatting-up of contestants. Whereas the winners of the TV game took away covetable consumer goods of the 1970s, *Have A Go* offered only the simplest of prizes like pots of jam and the odd shilling or two. The Barney in question was Barney Colehan, a BBC producer, who later went on to produce TV's *The Good Old Days* and *It's A Knockout*. Later Mabel supervised the prizes, hence the alternative 'Give him the money, Mabel' and the references to 'Mabel at the table'.

give order - thank you please! Colin Crompton's injunction to the members of Granada's *Wheeltappers And Shunters Social Club* (1974-7), of which he was the deadpan concert chairman. 'I had been including the character in my variety act for some years', Colin says, 'before Johnny Hamp of Granada TV suggested that we build a sketch round it for inclusion in the stage version of *The Comedians*. This led to *Wheeltappers*. Like most successful catchphrases it was not manufactured. It has been used by club concert chairmen for years - and still is. I suppose it was the exaggerated accent and facial expression which helped it "catch on".'

give over! Northern expression given widespread appeal by Al Read.

glad we could get together! Sign-off by John Cameron Swayze, American radio and TV newscaster of the 1940s and 50s. His customary opening was: 'And a good evening to you!'

goodbye and good love! Sign-off by Kid Jensen, the disc-jockey.

good evening, England! (This is Gillie Potter speaking to you in English) Potter's radio talks, delivered with an assumed pedagogic and superior air, recounted the doings of the Marshmallow family of Hogsnorton Towers - a delight from the 1940s and early 1950s, now alas, absent from the air. He would conclude with 'Goodbye, England, and good luck!' This reminds me of my own favourite broadcasting memory. When Radio 1 was introduced in 1967 the BBC had yet to cultivate newsreaders who could fit in with the prevailing tone of the station. As I recall it, on the very first day, someone not a million miles from Alvar Liddell was given the job of reading a news summary in the middle of a noisy rock show introduced by a DJ with the mandatory mid-Atlantic accent. The newsreader began: 'And now here is the news - *in English*.')

good evening, everyone! The customary greeting of A J Alan, radio storyteller of the 1920s and '30s. He was a civil servant (real name: Leslie Lambert) who eschewed personal publicity and always broadcast wearing a dinner-jacket. He never went into a studio without having a candle by him in case the lights fused.

good evening, Mr and Mrs North America and all the ships at sea. (Let's go to press!) Walter Winchell's peculiar (and variable) greeting to listeners of his Sunday night radio programme. The voice of America's most notorious gossip columnist also gave the rasping narration on the old TV series, *The Untouchables*. Born 1892, Winchell died in 1972.

good evening, young sir! Eric Morecambe's customary address to a girl.

good game . . . good game! Encouragement to contestants in the

Generation Game from its host, Bruce Forsyth.

(a) good idea, son! Max Bygraves in *Educating Archie* - also in another radio show, *Paradise Street,* and incorporated in a familiar song. Max was one of a long line of tutors to Archie Andrews, ventriloquist Peter Brough's dummy. Bizarre though the notion is of a radio ventriloquist, the programme (first broadcast on 6 June 1950) ran for many years.

good morning, boys! Opening line of Will Hay (1888-1949), 'headmaster of St Michael's', to which his pupils would reply wearily, 'Good morning, sir!'

good morning! / nice day! Exchange between Tommy Handley and Clarence Wright, as the commercial traveller who never seemed to sell anything, in *ITMA*.
Wright: Good morning!
Handley: Good morning!
Wright: Nice day!
Handley: Very!

good morning, sir! was there something? Sam Costa's entry line in *Much Binding In The Marsh,* reflecting his role as a kind of batman to Kenneth Horne and Richard Murdoch.

good neet! 'And so we come to the end of this week's *Have A Go,* which came to you from Blackburn, with Violet Carson at the piano. This is your old pal, Wilfred Pickles, wishing you all good luck and good neet!' Chorus of 'Come round any old time and make yourself at home.' End of programme!
Pickles had first, however, put this northern expression in the nation's ears

during his brief and controversial stint as a radio newsreader. Brendan Bracken at the wartime Ministry of Information had concluded that a voice such as that of Pickles would be less easy for the Germans to copy, so he was bought in and on one occasion ended the news (which till then had been read in God-like Oxbridge tones) with, 'Goodnight everybody - and to all northerners wherever you may be, good neet!'

goodness gracious me! The key phrase in Peter Sellers's Indian doctor impersonation to which all citizens of the subcontinent seem to aspire. It first occurred in a song recorded by Sellers and Sophia Loren based on their parts in the film of Shaw's *The Millionairess*.

goodnight and good luck! The sign-off line of Ed Murrow, the American broadcaster. Also, **Listen to Murrow tomorrow!**

goodnight and I love you all! (preceded by: 'thank you for watching my little show here tonight') Janet Webb's sign-off line during a series of the *Morecambe And Wise Show* on BBC TV. Buxom Janet would appear at the very end of the show, in which she had played no other part, and momentarily upstage Eric and Ernie by flinging her arms out wide and intoning these words in her diminutive voice.

goodnight, children, everywhere! Farewell from BBC radio *Children's Hour,* particularly as uttered by 'Uncle Mac' (Derek McCulloch) when many of the programme's listeners were evacuees.

goodnight, everybody . . . goodnight! Distinctive pay-off at the end of the day's radio from Stuart Hibberd (even in the days when announcers were anonymous). He would count four after saying 'goodnight, everybody' in order that listeners could say 'goodnight' to him, if they felt like it.

goodnight gentlemen, and good sailing! A rare example of informality from a BBC announcer in the starchier days of radio presentation - Frank Phillips's customary ending to a shipping forecast.

goodnight, Mrs Calabash, wherever you are! Splendidly obscure farewell from Jimmy 'Schnozzle' Durante.

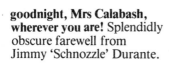

good old Charlieee! Richard Murdoch's interjection from *Much Binding In The Marsh*.

groovy baby! Quintessential 1960s expression given added impetus by its use on Radio 1 by disc-jockey Dave Cash. He would play a brief recording of a baby's voice saying it. In fact, the baby referred to as Microbe was Ian Doody, son of a BBC producer, Pat Doody. 'Groovy baby' stickers were much in demand in 1967-8, and Blue Mink put Microbe on to disc.

happy days! from *Band Waggon,* Askey and Murdoch in unison, reminiscing about their early days in the flat on top of Broadcasting House.

has he been in, whack? (See **'as 'e bin' in, whack?)**

hasn't it been a funny day, today? Ken Platt on radio's *Variety Fanfare* (early 1950s).

have a gorilla! Neddie Seagoon's offer of a cigarette in *The Goon Show,* to which the inevitable reply was 'No, thank you, I'm trying to give them up' or 'No, thanks, I only smoke baboons!'

have gun - will travel! Availability, as signalled in old newspaper personal columns, given wider currency by the phrase's use as the title of an American TV series.

have you ever had any embarrassing moments? Wilfred Pickles fishing for folksy laughs among contestants on *Have A Go.* After all, this was what the programme set out to provide: 'a spot of homely fun, presenting the people to the people'.

hello, folks! When Arthur Askey used this expression in the first *Band Waggon* broadcast in 1938 he received a call from Tommy Handley telling him to lay off, as Handley considered it to be *his* catchphrase. Askey coined 'hello, playmates!' instead and Handley continued to use 'hello, folks!' throughout *ITMA,* after which the Goons took up the cry and gave it a strangled delivery. Harry Secombe extended this to 'Hello, folks and what about the workers?' and Eric Morecambe gave it an almost sexual connotation by referring to 'a touch of hello folks and what about the workers!'

hello, good evening and welcome! David Frost's greeting, which contrives to say three things where only one is needed. Now an essential part of the Frost-impersonator's kit.

hello, honky-tonks! Clarence, the camp gentleman played by Dick Emery.

hello, it's me - Twinkletoes! Usually preceded by heavy footsteps. Bernard Bresslaw's 'thicko' greeting on *Educating Archie*. Following his success as the gormless private in *The Army Game* it was only natural that he should become one of Archie's educators!

hello, Jim! (pronounced 'Jeem' and/or sung) Spike Milligan's Jim Spriggs in *The Goon Show*.

hello, Mrs! A hangover from his days as a travelling hardware salesman and now a staple ingredient of Ken Dodd's act.

hello, my darlings! Charlie Drake's husky, baby-voiced greeting. (See also **'ello, darlin'!**)

hello, playmates! Arthur Askey's cry since the days of *Band Waggon*. Title of radio series. (See also **hello, folks!**)

hello, sailor! A difficult one to fathom, this. Safest to say that the phrase may always have been around but with varying amounts of heterosexual and homosexual emphasis (cf. the old naval saying: 'Ashore it's wine, women and song; aboard, it's rum, bum and concertina'). Spike Milligan claims to have given it a new lease of life on one of his *Q* TV shows - to fill up time he just said it over and over. Dudley Moore also used it, and the cast of radio's *I'm Sorry I'll Read That Again* promoted it heavily, perhaps influenced by there being a number of newsworthy sailors about at the time, such as Prince Philip, Prince Charles and Edward Heath.

hello . . . twins! Derek McCulloch and Mary Elizabeth Jenkin were Mac and Elizabeth among the original 'Uncles' and 'Aunts' on BBC radio *Children's Hour*. In the early days birthday greetings were read out (until they were dropped in 1932 because they took up nearly half the 'Hour') and their simultaneous cry of 'hello . . . twins!' or 'hello . . . triplets!' became a catchphrase. Miss Jenkin succeeded McCulloch as Head of *Children's Hour* in 1950.

here come de judge! Was much used in the late 1960s on *Rowan And Martin's Laugh-In*. It originated with a Negro vaudeville veteran, Dewey 'Pigmeat' Markham, to introduce a series of blackout sketches:
Judge: Have you ever been up before me?
Defendant: I don't know - what time do you get up?
Pigmeat himself appeared on *Laugh-In*.

here's a funny thing! 'Now this *is* a funny thing. I went home the other night . . .

there's a funny thing!' Max Miller, 'the Cheeky Chappie', music-hall star who died in 1963 at the age of sixty-eight.

here's another fine mess you've gotten me into! (and variations upon the same). The anguished cry of Oliver Hardy to Stan Laurel which managed to register itself as a catchphrase with the public because there were sufficient Laurel and Hardy films to establish it.

here's Johnny! Said with a rising inflection on the first word, the announcer's distinctive introduction to Johnny Carson on NBC's *Tonight* show. This was emulated during Simon Dee's brief reign as a chat-show host in Britain during the 1960s. The studio audience joined in the rising inflection of the announcer's 'Simon'.

here's looking at you, kid! Humphrey Bogart to Ingrid Bergman in the film *Casablanca*. A quotation turned into a catchphrase by Bogart impersonators.

(and now) here's the man with the news of the present - the man to whom the news wouldn't be the news without the news -here's Dickie! Dan Rowan's nonsense introduction to Dick Martin in a segment of their *Laugh-In*.

here's to the next time! Henry Hall, the bandleader. It was the title of his signature tune and became the title of his autobiography.

here we are again! Greeting introduced by Joseph Grimaldi (Joey the Clown 1779—1837) and subsequently used by almost all clowns on entering the ring.

hern, hern! American noise by Harry
Secombe as 'Lootenant Hern-Hern' in *The
Goon Show,* described as 'an encapsulation
of the American language'.

he's a great guy! *ITMA.*

he's fallen in the water! Spoken by Little
Jim (Spike Milligan) in *The Goon Show.*
'Oh, dear children - look what's happened to
Uncle Harry!' Little Jim (helpfully, in simple
sing-song voice): 'He's fallen in the wa-ter!'

he's lovely, Mrs Hoskin, he's lovely! Ted
Ray as Ivy to Bob Pearson as Mrs Hoskin
in *Ray's A Laugh.* Ted Ray recalled in his
book *Raising The Laughs:* 'George Inns
(the producer) agreed that the climax of
their original conversation should be the
mention of a mystical "Dr Hardcastle"
whom Ivy secretly adored. We had
absolutely no inkling of how warmly the
listening millions were to take our new
voices to their hearts; but from the moment
Bob, in his new role, had spoken the
words, "I sent for young Dr Hardcastle,"
and we heard Ivy's excited little intake of
breath, followed by, "he's loo-vely, Mrs
Hoskin . . . he's loo-oo-lovely!" a new
phrase had come into being.'

he's one of Nature's! Martha about Albert
('Don't you insult my husband, he's . . .')
in *Ray's A Laugh.* Ted Ray numbered it
among the show's failed catchphrases.

he's very good, you know! A somewhat
double-edged compliment from *The Goon
Show.*

hi gang! Ben Lyon's greeting to the audience of his wartime BBC radio programme of the same name, first broadcast 26 May, 1940. He would call out 'Hi gang!' 'Hi, Ben!' would come the reply. At the end of the show, 'So long, gang!'/'So long, Ben!'

hi, sports fans! (accompanied by the tinkling of a bell) Alan Sues as an all-American TV sports presenter on *Laugh-In*.

hi-yo, Silver! 'A fiery horse with the speed of light . . . and a cloud of dust . . . and a hearty "hi-yo, Silver!" ' - the immortal introduction to the masked Lone Ranger and his horse, Silver, in the various radio and film accounts of their exploits, accompanied of course by the sound of Rossini's 'William Tell' overture. Groucho Marx used to say that George Seaton (who was the first Lone Ranger on American radio) invented the call 'Hi-yo, Silver!' because he was incapable of whistling to his horse. At this, the Lone Ranger's Indian friend, Tonto, might well have said of Groucho: 'Him bad man, kimos sabi!'

holy flypaper! ('holy cow!', 'holy felony!', 'holy geography!', 'holy schizophrenia!', 'holy haberdashery!', etc). The prefix 'holy' to any exclamation was particularly the province of Batman and Robin, characters created by Bob Kane and featured in best-selling comic books for over thirty years before they were portrayed by Adam West and Burt Ward in the TV film series.
Not to be confused with their other interjections: Pow! Biff! Oooff! Thwack! Crunch! Rakkk! Oooffff! and Bonk!

how about that then? Repetition phrase of BBC announcer Roger Moffat (after piece of music) during a long and fruitful relationship with the BBC Northern Dance Orchestra (formerly Northern Variety Orchestra) in Manchester, from the late 1950s to the early '60s.

how do you do? Said with a slight nod by Jimmy James. Also used by Arthur Askey, it became the title of a radio series in 1949. Terry-Thomas began his monologues (subsequently adapted for TV as, 'How do you view?') with it. (See also **Cardew do?**)

how's about that, then, guys and gals? Another of Jimmy Savile OBE's identity tags.

how's your father? The music-hall star, Harry Tate.

how's your poor (old) feet? Origin obscure - perhaps from nineteenth-century music-hall.

how tickled I am! 'I was once a salesman and I've always been fascinated by sales techniques,' says Ken Dodd, 'and catchphrases are like trade marks - they are attention-getting details which in my case make people exclaim, "Ah yes, Ken Dodd." The disadvantage of catchphrases is that they get worn - like tyres. So I devised "how tickled I am" as a phrase that could be varied by the addition of a joke, "have you ever been tickled, Mrs?" and so on.'

hush, keep it dark! Commander High-Price (Jon Pertwee) in Navy *Merry Go Round,* subsequently *Waterlogged Spa.*

I always do my best for all my gentlemen!
Mrs Lola Tickle (Maurice Denham)
appeared within six weeks of the start of
ITMA in 1939. As office charlady to Mr
ITMA (Tommy Handley), she was the
precursor by a full year of Mrs Mopp.

I am the greatest! Muhammad Ali
(formerly Cassius Clay) admits that he
acquired his 'I am the greatest . . . I am the
prettiest' routine from the wrestler,
Gorgeous George, whom he saw in Las
Vegas. 'I noticed they all paid to get in -and
I said, "This is a good idea!" ' On another
occasion, Ali admitted to a group of
schoolchildren: 'I'm not really the greatest.
I only say I'm the greatest because it sells
tickets.'

I brought this for you, sir! Mrs Mopp
(Dorothy Summers) giving her customary
present to Tommy Handley in *ITMA*.

I can hear you! A Charlie Chester
catchphrase. He recalls: ' "I can hear you"
was one of those things that started off in
the rehearsal room because somebody was
talking about me and I suddenly said, "I
can hear you!" and I found myself saying it
again when all the stars of the shows in
Yarmouth had to go to one of the piers to
do a midnight-matinée show as a sort of
final tribute to the town. After my show I
made my way up to the theatre, where the
show was already in progress. Tommy
Trinder was on stage doing his party piece
and as I walked in the darkness down the
gangway I heard him talk about me, so I
yelled out "I can hear you!" and he was
surprised to know I was there listening to
him. The audience fell about laughing so
we stuck that in my show when somebody
was running another person down.'

I'd do anything for the wife! *ITMA*.

I didn't get where I am today . . . ! The frequent musing of C.J. in television's *The Rise And Fall of Reginald Perrin*.

I didn't oughter 'ave et it! (or 'you didn't oughter . . .') Jack Warner in his book *Jack Of All Trades* recounts the occasion when he was leaving Broadcasting House in London with Richard Murdoch: 'I had to step over the legs of a couple of fellows who were sitting in the sunshine with their backs against the wall eating their lunches from paper bags. As we passed, I heard one say to the other, "I don't know what my old woman has given me for dinner today but I didn't oughter 'ave et it." I remarked to Dickie, "If that isn't a cue for a song, I don't know what is!" It provided me with my first catchphrase to be picked out by members of the public.'

I do not like this game! Peter Sellers as Bluebottle in *The Goon Show*.
Seagoon: Now, Bluebottle, take this stick of dynamite.
Bluebottle: No, I do not like this game!

I don't mind if I do! The immortal catchphrase of Colonel Chinstrap (Jack Train) in *ITMA*. It first appeared in 1940-41 in the form, 'Thanks, I will!' in response to a slight suggestion of liquid refreshment. The original Colonel was an elderly friend of John Snagge's - a typical ex-Indian army type, well pleased with himself. The phrase had been in existence long before. *Punch* carried a cartoon in 1880 with the following caption:

Porter: Virginia Water!

Bibulous old gentleman (seated in a railway carriage): Gin and water! I don't mind if I do!

ITMA, however, secured the phrase's place in the language, as the Colonel doggedly turned every hint into an offer:

Handley: Hello, what's this group? King John signing the Magna Carta at Runnymede?

Chinstrap: Rum and mead, sir? I don't mind if I do!

I don't suppose it'll matter! Another *Band Waggon* phrase, as when Askey and Murdoch were stirring a Christmas pudding in the bath - 'Will it leave a mark? Oh, I don't suppose it'll matter!'

I don't wan't to hear about it! A repetition line from Dan Rowan and Dick Martin's routine in *Laugh-In*. Martin is endlessly on the look-out for 'action' while Rowan can hardly keep his partner's mind off sex:

Rowan (fretting about Martin's frail appearance): For your own good, you should pick up some weight.

Martin: Shoulda been with me last night. I picked up 118 pounds.

Rowan: I don't want to hear about it . . .

Martin: It was for my own good, too!

I don't wish to know that - kindly leave the stage! The traditional response to a joke, given a new lease of life by *The Goon Show* and other British entertainments which still owe so much to the routines and spirit of music hall. (See also **I say, I say, I say!**)

if it's h-h-hokay with you, it's h-h-hokay with me! The stuttering catchphrase of one Tubby Turner, Lancashire music-hall artist, born 1882.

I forgot the question! A repetition phrase from Goldie Hawn, at one time the resident blonde dum-dum of *Laugh-In*. In the middle of a quick exchange she would giggle and then miaow 'I forgot the question!' At first her fluffs were a case of misreading cue cards, then they became part of her act.

if you haven't been to Manchester, you haven't lived! As true today as it was when uttered regularly by Tommy Trafford (Graham Stark) in *Ray's A Laugh*.

if you want anything, just whistle! Not a genuine catchphrase, perhaps, but hovering near. It is from the famous speech by Lauren Bacall to Humphrey Bogart in their first film together *To Have And Have Not* and may now, I suppose, have acquired some additional magic from their subsequent real-life association. Bacall as Slim says to Bogart as Steve: 'You know

you don't have to act with me, Steve. You
don't have to say anything, and you don't
have to do anything - not a thing. Or
maybe just whistle. You know how to
whistle don't you, Steve? You just put your
lips together and blow.'

if you want anything, ring me! Jimmy
Logan, in the Scottish radio series *It's All
Yours, circa* 1952.

I go - I come back! Said in a hoarse whisper
by Ali Oop (Horace Percival), the saucy
postcard vendor in *ITMA*. First used in the
summer of 1940.

I hate yew! Dick Emery as Grimble in
Educating Archie.

I hate you, Butler! Said by the Inspector
(Stephen Lewis) in the ITV series *On The Buses*.

I jus kum up fer Dorset! Billy Burden.

I just don't care any more! Larry Grayson,
after doing something cheeky.

I'll 'ave to ask me Dad! The point of this
ITMA catchphrase was that it was spoken
by a character who sounded about a
hundred years of age called The Ancient
Mark Time. Randolph Churchill speaking
at a general election meeting in 1945 was
heckled with the remark, 'He'll have to ask
his Dad!'

I'll be leaving you now, sir! (with hand
anticipating tip) Bill Fraser as Sergeant-
Major Claud Snudge in ITV's *Bootsie and
Snudge*.

I'll do anything for money! This expression
used in various forms by Eli Woods in

Radio 2's *The Show With Ten Legs*
(accompanied by the ring of a cash
register), seems to me to have all the
makings of a good catchphrase.

I'll drink to that! Basically North American
way of showing agreement, given further
currency in *Laugh-In*.

I'll forget my own name in a minute! The
nameless Man from the Ministry (played by
Horace Percival) in *ITMA*.

I'll give it foive! A real rarity - a
catchphrase launched by a member of the
public. Not that Janice Nicholls, a Brum
girl conscripted on to the pop jury of
ABC's *Thank Your Lucky Stars,* could
avoid a peculiar form of celebrity for long.
Awarding votes to new releases in her local
dialect and declaring (as if in mitigation for
some awful vocal performance), 'But I like
the backing!' she became a minor celebrity
and even made a record herself called - wait
for it - 'I'll give it five' c/w 'The
Wednesbury Madison' . . . of which almost
everyone else declared, 'I'll give it about
minus five.'

(well) I'll go to the foot of our stairs! Old
northern expression used by Tommy
Handley in *ITMA,* etc.

I'll have a half! Jacko in the ITV series
Love Thy Neighbour.

I'll separate you from your breath! A
favourite expression of Norman Evans, the
north country comedian.

I'll smash your face in! Eric Morecambe.

I love that gag! The American (sometimes

referred to as 'Al K. Traz') played by Peter Sellers in *Ray's A Laugh*.

I'm absolutely fed up! Monica (Beryl Reid) in *Educating Archie*.

I'm dreaming oh my darling love of thee! Cyril Fletcher recalls that he was persuaded to broadcast 'Dreaming of Thee', a poem by Edgar Wallace, in 1938. He did it in an extraordinary voice - a cockney caricature -and the constant refrain at the end of each verse, 'I'm dreaming oh my darling love of thee', got yells of delight. It 'made' him, he says, and later when he returned to London for a repeat performance he was on a bus and the conductor was saying 'Dreaming of thee' to every passenger with a passable imitation of Fletcher's funny voice as he gave them their tickets!

I meanter say! George Robey.

I mean that most sincerely, friends! Hughie Greene was always saying, 'sincerely, friends' when he compèred his TV talent show *Opportunity Knocks,* but Mike Yarwood claims to have invented this precise formulation for his impersonation of Greene. A case of art imitating art, perhaps.

I'm free! The lilting cry of Mr Humphries (John Inman), the lighter-than-air menswear salesman of Grace Bros store in the BBC TV series *Are You Being Served?*

I'm going down now, sir! *ITMA's* Diver (Horace Percival) - see **don't forget the diver!** I'm told that bomber pilots in the Second World War would use this phrase when about to make a descent. From the VE day edition of *ITMA:*

EFFECTS: KNOCKING

Tommy Handley: Who's that knocking on the tank?

The Diver: Don't forget the diver, sir -don't forget the diver.

Tommy Handley: Lumme, it's Deepend Dan. Listen, as the war's over, what are you doing?

The Diver: I'm going down now, sir.

EFFECTS: BUBBLES

I'm going to make him an offer he can't refuse! Wherever this phrase originated, it became famous as a direct result of its inclusion in Mario Puzo's novel *The Godfather* and in the film. A singer/actor is after a film part and seeks help from Don Corleone (played memorably by Marlon Brando with his mouth stuffed full of cotton wool or orange peel): 'In a month from now this Hollywood big shot's going to give you what you want,' the Godfather confides. 'Too late,' says the singer. 'They start shooting in a week.' The Godfather affirms: 'I'm going to make him an offer he can't refuse.'

I'm in charge! During Bruce Forsyth's time as compère of the ATV show *Sunday Night At The London Palladium,* he was supervising 'Beat the Clock', a game involving members of the public. A young couple were in a muddle, throwing plates at a see-saw table. Bruce said, 'Hold on a minute . . . I'm in charge!' and the audience laughed. Lapel badges began appearing with the slogan, foremen had it painted on their hard hats. The phrase suited Brucie's mock-bossy manner to a tee. The show - with a series of compères - ran from 1954-65.

I'm looking for someone to love! The

honest lament of Arthur Fallowfield, the loam-rich-voiced countryman, played by Kenneth Williams, in *Beyond Our Ken*.

I'm mortified! Jimmy 'Schnozzle' Durante.

I'm no mug! According to Ernie Wise, a catchphrase used 'years ago' by himself and Eric Morecambe.

I'm not stupid, you know! Bernard Bresslaw as Bernard, Archie's tutor, in *Educating Archie*. 'This phrase came up spontaneously,' he recalls, 'because it was entirely in character.'

I'm only here for the beer! From an advertisement for Double Diamond. (See **nice one, Cyril!**)

I'm sorry, I'll read that again! The newsreader's traditional apology turned into a cliché, if not a catchphrase, by its being used as the title of the BBC radio comedy show.

I'm worried about Jim! Ellis Powell as the eponymous heroine of radio's *Mrs Dale's Diary,* (referring to her doctor husband). Although she may not have uttered the phrase very often, it was essential in parodies of the programme.

indubitably! The characteristic utterance of Robertson Hare (1891-1979). He entitled his autobiography *Yours Indubitably*.

(ee) in't it grand to be daft! Albert Modley, the north-country comedian who died in 1979 at the age of eighty-seven, achieved nation-wide fame through radio's *Variety Bandbox*. A former railway porter, he employed several northern expressions, including: 'heee!' and 'flippin' 'eck!'

I only arsked! Quite the most popular
catchphrase of the late 1950s. Bernard
Bresslaw played a large, gormless private
-'Popeye' Popplewell - in Granada TV's
Army Game (1957-62) and this was his
response whenever someone put him down.
The phrase occurred in the very first
episode and a story is told of the day when
the *Army Game* team first realised they had
a catchphrase on their hands. It is said that
Milo Lewis, the director, was rehearsing a
scene in which the lads from Hut 29
realised that though they had been moved
to a new camp they still had not escaped the
clutches of their sergeant-major (played
by William Hartnell). 'Quite a reunion!' he
commented. 'Can we bring girls?' the
Bresslaw character inquired. 'No, you
can't,' replied the sergeant-major. 'I only
arsked!' At this point, Milo Lewis is said to
have exclaimed enthusiastically, 'We've got
a catchphrase!' The others chorused, 'You
mean . . . ?' 'Yes,' replied Lewis, 'Can we
bring girls'!

irky perky! *Rowan and Martin's Laugh-In.*

I say, I say, I say! Hard to say whether
Murray and Mooney, the variety duo,
invented this interruption but they
perfected the routine in their act during the
1930s. Mooney would interrupt with, 'I
say, I say, I say!' To whatever he had to
impart, Murray would reply 'I don't wish
to know that - kindly leave the stage!'
Harry Murray died in 1967, Harry Mooney
in 1972.

I say, what a smasher! A Charlie Chester
phrase from the post-war radio show *Stand
Easy*. Charlie recalls: 'It was really a joke
on my missus. My wife broke her arm and
was sitting in the audience of *Stand Easy*.

She's got this great big plaster and she was a blonde girl and I told Len Marten to keep coming up to me with the line "I say, what a smasher!" Then we would carry on as if nothing had happened. He'd come back later with "I say, what a smasher!" and then at the end of the programme, the resolving gag was: "Len, what do you mean by all this 'I say, what a smasher' business?" He said, "The blonde in the third row!" And there's this broken arm sticking out like a beacon. The entire audience looked at Mum and fell about laughing. Strangely enough I went down to a Butlin holiday camp not long after and somebody dropped a pile of crockery. Of course the noise resounded all over the place and everybody shouted "I say, what a smasher!" Everybody laughed and that became a catchphrase.'

I say, you fellows! Billy Bunter's famous cry from Frank Richards's Greyfriars stories - given a memorably metallic ring in Gerald Campion's brilliant TV characterisation in the 1950s. Also, **oh, crikey!** and **Yaroooo!**

I seen 'im! Cyril (Peter Sellers) in *The Goon Show*.

isn't he a panic? A submerged catchphrase from radio's *The Burkiss Way* - by which I mean that it was known only to cast and writers. But there it was in the dialogues between Fred Harris and Eric Pode of Croydon (Chris Emmett).

it all depends what you mean by . . . C E M Joad - often called 'Professor' though he was not entitled to be - was one of the regulars in BBC radio's *Brains Trust,* first broadcast in 1941, which Kenneth Clark, another regular, describes as 'a form of popular entertainment second only to Tommy Handley'. Joad (born in 1891) was, according to Clark, 'a quick-witted, bumptious disciple of Bertrand Russell, who treated the *Brains Trust* as a competitive sport and a chance of showing off'.

His technique was to jump in first and leave the other speakers with little else to say. Alternatively, he would try and undermine arguments by using the phrase with which he became famous. When the Chairman once read out a question from a listener, Mr W E Jack of Keynsham - 'Are thoughts things or about things?' - Joad inevitably began his answer with 'It all depends what you mean by a "thing".'

Joad's broadcasting fame ended rather abruptly when he was found travelling by rail using a ticket that was not valid. The BBC banished him. He died in 1953.

I thank you! (See ay thang yew!)

I think the answer lies in the soil! A line created by Barry Took and Eric Merriman for Kenneth Williams in *Beyond Our Ken.* The character was that of a ruminative professional countryman (perhaps based on Ralph Wightman or A G Street) called Arthur Fallowfield who appeared in an *Any Questions* take-off.

it don't arf make you larf! Max Wall -almost a catchphrase.

it is disgraceful - it ought not to be allowed! Mr Grouser in the radio *Children's Hour* feature, *Toytown.*

it'll be all right with a bit of doing up! Arthur Askey in *Band Waggon,* doing up the flat at the top of Broadcasting House. 'Shall we throw this out? No, it'll be all right with a bit of doing up!'

it's a bird, it's a plane, it's . . . ! From the early radio and film versions of Superman's exploits (sometimes expressed as a question: 'is it a bird? is it a plane?'). The full introductory announcement went like this (provide your own sound effects): 'Faster than a speeding bullet! More powerful than a locomotive! Able to leap tall buildings at a single bound! Look! Up in the sky! It's a bird! It's a plane! It's Superman! Yes, it's Superman! - strange visitor from another planet, who came to earth with powers and abilities far beyond those of mortal men. Superman! - who can change the course of mighty rivers, bend steel in his bare hands, and who (disguised as Clark Kent, mild-mannered reporter for a great metropolitan newspaper) fights a never-ending battle for truth, justice and the American way!'

it's all been happening this week! Stock phrase of Norman Vaughan during his TV Palladium days (from 1962) . . .

it's all in the mind, you know! Convincing explanation of anything heard in *The Goon Show* - often said by the announcer, Wallace Greenslade.

it's being so cheerful as keeps me going! Said by Mona Lott (Joan Harben), the gloomy laundrywoman in *ITMA*. When told to keep her pecker up by Tommy Handley, she would reply, 'I always do, sir, it's being so cheerful . . .' Her family was always running into bad luck so she had plenty upon which to exercise her cheerfulness.

it's daft! Norman Evans.

it's goodnight from me / And it's goodnight from him! Ronnie Corbett and Ronnie Barker, sending up the contrived way TV co-presenters can sign off, in their BBC TV series *The Two Ronnies.*

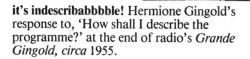

it's indescribabbbble! Hermione Gingold's response to, 'How shall I describe the programme?' at the end of radio's *Grande Gingold, circa* 1955.

it's make-your-mind-up time! Phrase from Hughie Greene's *Opportunity Knocks,* meaning the point where the viewers had to decide which was the best act in the talent contest.

it's me noives! Lefty (played by Jack Train) in *ITMA.*

it sends me! Having established the toothsome, faintly posh schoolgirl, Monica, in *Educating Archie,* Beryl Reid wanted to find another character from a different social class. This turned out to be Marlene (pronounced 'Marleen') from Birmingham, complete with Brum accent and girl friend Deirdre. She helped establish what was in any case an archetypal 1950s phrase for the effect of music on the hearts and minds of the young.

it's terrific! Pronounced 'turreefeek' by Marlene (see above).

it's that man again! It is appropriate that *ITMA,* the radio programme which included more catchphrases per square second than any other, before or since, should have had as it's title an acronym based on a catchphrase. 'It's that man again!' was a late 1930s expression, often used in newspaper headlines, for Adolf Hitler, who was always bursting into the news with some territorial claim or other.

it's the way I tell 'em! (You've heard them all before, but . . .) Frank Carson, the Ulster comedian.

it's turned out nice again! George Formby disclaimed any credit for originating the phrase with which he always opened his act and which became the title of one of his films in 1941. 'It's simply a familiar Lancashire expression,' he once said. 'People use it naturally up there. I used it as part of a gag and have been doing so ever since' - particularly in films after emerging from some disaster or other. It is also the title of a song.

(ee,) it was agony, Ivy! Said by Mrs Hoskin (Bob Pearson) to Ivy (Ted Ray) in *Ray's A Laugh*. May have stemmed originally from the music halls. (See also **he's lovely, Mrs Hoskin, he's lovely!**)

I've arrived - and to prove it, I'm here! 'I had the whole country saying things like this,' claims Max Bygraves with justification. The catchphrase arose during his time on *Educating Archie* and formed part of his 'bill-matter' when he appeared at the Palladium in 1952.

I've been sponned! This phrase does not actually occur in the episode of *The Goon Show* called 'The Spon Plague', broadcast in March 1958, but I clearly remember my school friends at the time uttering the phrase. The symptoms of sponning included bare knees - of which we had quite a few in those days.

I've failed! Scots comedian, Dave Willis (died 1973). In a Sherlock Holmes sketch he used to slope on stage with a huge magnifying glass. Peering through it, he would go up to an imaginary flower and without bending his knees would balance and hover over it, examining it through the glass, getting closer and closer until he fell over. 'I've failed,' he'd wail in a wee voice.

I've got a letter from a bloke in Bootle! Jimmy James.

I've got a million of 'em! A bridge between jokes used by both Max Miller and Jimmy 'Schnozzle' Durante.

I've lost all my faith in human nature! Charles Leno as Dear old Dad in *Ray's A Laugh*.

I've not been well! George Williams.

I wanna tell you a story! A fascinating example of a catchphrase being wished on performer by impersonator. Max Bygraves may have said it once or twice (with the appropriate hand-shaking gestures) but Mike Yarwood claims to have singled it out. Now Bygraves himself uses the phrase in self-parody and even as the title of his autobiography. Still, as he says, he once went into a competition for Max Bygraves impressions - and came fifth!

I want to be alone! Garbo claims that what she said was 'I want to be *let* alone', and -as Alexander Walker remarks in his book *Sex in the Movies* - no trace can be found in any of the publicity surrounding her early Hollywood days of the phrase with which she is associated. However, even she saw fit to utter it in various films before succumbing completely to her desire for privacy.

I was amazed! Frankie Howerd explains that when he was starting in radio just after the war he thought a good gimmick would be for him to give unusual emphasis to certain words. Hence 'I was a-*mazed*' and 'ladies and gentle-*men*'. George Robey also used to say, 'I'm more than surprised - I'm amazed.'

I was livid! Grimble (Dick Emery) in *Educating Archie* would usually spin this out - 'Oh, I was livid . . . livid I was . . . I wasn't half livid . . . I was!'

I was there! Max Boyce.

I wish I had as many shillings! Said by Tommy Handley in *ITMA* in response to a remark such as 'now I have a million eggs'. This was a conscious borrowing from Jimmy Learmouth, a northern comedian of Handley's youth.

I won't take me coat off - I'm not stopping! Ken Platt, the nasal-voiced, slightly lugubrious northern comedian, was handed this catchphrase on a plate by Ronnie Taylor, producer of radio's *Variety Fanfare* in January 1951. Says Ken, I told him rather grudgingly that I thought it was as good as anything . . . and I've been stuck with it ever since. People are disappointed if I don't say it. I tease them and pretend not to know what they're talking about if they ask me to "say it"!'

Jennifer! Said in a little girl voice by Bob Pearson in *Ray's A Laugh:*
Jennifer: Hello!
George (Ted Ray): Why, it's a little girl. What's your name?
Jennifer: Jen-nif-fer!
I can remember people at the time (mid-1950s) saying 'My name's Jennifer' so perhaps this was another formulation of the phrase.

John Henry, come here! / Coming, Blossom! In the 1920s, John Henry became the first wireless comedian, playing a henpecked Yorkshireman with a domineering wife, Blossom.

John Willie, come on! George Formby senior (who died in 1921) included in his act a typical Lancashire character called 'John Willie'. The phrase 'swept the country'. Audiences waited for the line and knew just when it was coming - so they could join in:
We went to Madame Two-Sword's waxwork show and it were grand, And there we saw all t'waxworks, kings and queens all shakin' hands,
There was Mary Queen of Scots and Queen Elizabeth you see - They rather took my fancy when the wife said to me: 'John Willie, come on! It's closin' time, you see.' The lights went out and all was dark an' quiet as could be. On turnin' round to my surprise I found the wife had gone, And I'm sure I heard Queen Elizabeth say, 'John Willie, come on!'

jolly hockey sticks! Nowadays mainly used in an adjectival sense to describe a type of woman - public school, games-playing, enthusiastic - but originally an expression used by Monica, Archie's schoolgirl friend, in *Educating Archie*. Coined by Beryl Reid, the actress, who modestly proclaims: 'I can't write comedy material . . . but I know what sort of thing my characters should say!' In this case she lighted upon a masterly phrase which has passed into the language.

just like that! Tommy Cooper has been using this phrase for as long as he can remember. It was not a premeditated catchphrase. He only noticed it when impressionists and others singled it out from his act. Said in the appropriate gruff tones and accompanied by small paddling gestures, it is of course a gift to mimics. Inevitably the phrase is used by Cooper as the title of his autobiography. There is also a song incorporating it.

just watch it, that's all! Eric Morecambe admonishing Little Ern and grabbing him by the lapels.

kissy, kissy! Miss Piggy, the porcine vamp and Kermit-crusher on *The Muppet Show*.

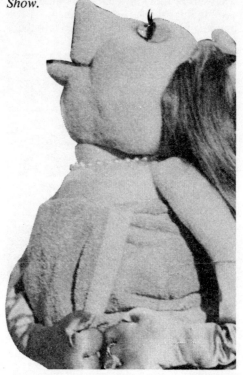

ladies and gentlemen! One of the phrases to which Frankie Howerd always gives unusual emphasis.

large lumps! Expression used by Dickie Hassett, who flourished *circa* 1940 (He was even given a radio show with this title — though I think I must have missed it!)

learn a trade! A much-repeated phrase of Old Wal from the Buildings (Wallas Eaton) in *Take It From Here*. 'We're very proud of Jim back in the Buildings,' he would say (of Jimmy Edwards), but he was always exhorting Jim to come on home and learn a trade so that at least when he was out of work he would know what sort of work he was out of.

left hand down a bit! Leslie Phillips doing a spot of navigating in *The Navy Lark*.

let me tell you! *Happidrome* popularised this expression during the Second World War. In every episode, Enoch would say at least once, 'Let me tell you, Mr Lovejoy!' before revealing some startling fact.

let's get on with it! Nat Mills and Bobbie were a variety act that flourished in the 1930s and '40s portraying 'a gumpish type of lad and his equally gumpish girl friend'. Nat recalls: 'It was during the very early part of the war. We were booked by the BBC to go to South Wales for a *Worker's Playtime.* Long tables had been set up in front of the stage for the workers to have lunch before the broadcast. On this occasion a works foreman went round all the tables shouting, "Come on, let's get on with it", to get them to finish their lunch on time. I was informed he used this phrase so many times the workers would mimic him among themselves. So I said to Bobbie, "You start the broadcast by talking to yourself and I'll interject and say, 'Let's get on with it'." Lo and behold it got such a yell of laughter we kept it in all our broadcasts. Even Churchill used our slogan to the troops during the early part of the war.'

light the blue touchpaper and retire immediately! The firework instruction used as a catchphrase by Arthur Askey in *Band Waggon* on Guy Fawkes Night and used subsequently when withdrawing from confrontation with Mrs Bagwash.

listen! Frankie Howerd. 'Now listen, brethren, before we begin the Eisteddfod . . . !'

little gel! Jack Warner to Joan Winters, with whom he used to exchange saucy chat in *Garrison Theatre*.

(a) little of what you fancy does you good! Marie Lloyd from a song.

look that up in your Funk and Wagnalls! *Laugh-In* referring to the American dictionary.

lovely grub, lovely grub! Said by George Gorge (played by Fred Yule) in *ITMA*. 'The greediest man ever to have two ration books' used to say it, smacking his lips - as also did Charles Hill during his stint as the Radio Doctor (without smacking his lips).

lover boy! Pat Coombs as Ursula In *Ray's A Laugh, circa* 1960.

love you madly! Duke Ellington used to say, 'We'd like you to know that the boys in the band all love you madly!' - also the title of one of his songs.

Mabel at the table! (See **give him the money, Barney!**)

magic! Bill Maynard as Selwyn Froggit in the Yorkshire TV series *Oh No, It's Selwyn Froggit!*

many, many times! Innuendo from Lady Beatrice Counterblast (née Clissold) (played by Betty Marsden) in *Round The Horne,* originally referring to the number of times she had been married. Barry Took, co-scriptwriter with Marty Feldman, recalls an audience at *The Sound Of Music* falling about when the phrase was used in all seriousness during the run of the radio show.

(a) martini - shaken, not stirred! James Bond's classic piece of drink snobbery occurs first in the film *Goldfinger.* Having narrowly escaped being sawn in two by a laser-beam, he awakes to find himself on a plane with Pussy Galore. An oriental girl offers him a drink and he makes this specification - not one devised by Ian Fleming but by the screenwriters.

mastermind! Mrs Easy the home-help (Patricia Hayes) in *Ray's A Laugh, circa* 1954. 'Now don't you take that tone of voice with me, Mastermind!'

(a) mauve one! Frank Muir describes this *Take It From Here* catchphrase as 'the genuine article . . . a meaningless phrase, first used by Jimmy Edwards when selecting a wine-gum and given such a risible inflection by Jim ("a *mauve* one") that Denis Norden and I worked it into a vast number of shows thereafter to describe (for example) a stamp, a businessman's face, a suit, etc. This is almost a perfect example of a catchphrase in that it was not imposed upon the listeners but chosen by them to be a catchphrase.'

Jimmy Edwards recalled an occasion in May 1952 when, as Rector of Aberdeen University, he went to Buckingham Palace. A courtier remarked that Jim's academic robe was magnificent but that he should do a swap with the Dean of Westminster, who was also present. When Jim asked why, the courtier replied, 'His is a *mauve* one!'

meet the wife - don't laugh! Dave Morris.

Meredith, we're in! Shout of triumph which originated in a music-hall sketch 'The Bailiff' (or 'Moses and Son'), performed by Fred Kitchen, the leading comedian of Fred Karno's company, and first produced in 1907. The phrase was used each time a bailiff and his assistant looked like gaining entrance to a house. (I am told that Fred Kitchen even has it on his gravestone!)

migraine! From a letter to the London *Evening News* (17 February 1978): 'May I ask Mike Reid to drop his latest catchphrase "migraine" whenever he gets a burst of applause? I would have written earlier but I have been in a blacked-out room for eight days suffering from a migraine attack. In 30 years, migraine has caused enough havoc in my life without a comedian trying to make it a laughing-matter, which it isn't. Mrs H K, Putney.'

mind how you go! Given a new lease of life by Jack Warner in *Dixon Of Dock Green*.

mind my bike! In his autobiography, *Jack Of All Trades,* Jack Warner writes thus of the catchphrase he used when making an entrance on *Garrison Theatre,* tinkling a bike bell as he did so: 'When I dropped the phrase for two weeks, I had 3,000 letters from listeners asking why . . . the only other complaint came from a father who wrote, ''I am very keen on your *Garrison Theatre* show and I like the comedy very much, but I have spent several hundreds of pounds on my son's education and all he can do is shout 'Mind my bike!' in a very raucous Cockney voice. I'm trying to break him of the habit so will you please stop saying it?''

Warner also recalls that when his producer, Charles Shadwell, was once fined at Bristol for causing an obstruction with his car, his solicitor pleaded: 'Mr Shadwell became engrossed in conversation with Mr Jack Warner . . . they were discussing that gentleman's bicycle, about which you have no doubt heard.'

mine's a persico! Said by Jack Train as Funf in *ITMA*. 'I think it's positively persico!'

missed him! *ITMA*.

morning! Ed Stewart's customary falsetto greeting on radio's *Junior Choice* from about 1971 onwards. Like his farewell 'byeee!' it echoes the way children say these words.

most irregular, most irregular! Jack Train as Fusspot, the burlesque civil servant in *ITMA*.

Mr Handley . . . Mr Handley! Miss Hotchkiss in *ITMA*.

Mrs Ginocchi, SOS! Arthur Lucan, who used to appear as Old Mother Riley with his wife, Kitty McShane, in music-hall.

mum, mum, they are laughing at me! Arthur English in his late-1940s incarnation as a wide boy with an outsize tie. Arthur recalls: 'On my entrance during my first broadcast I had my big tie rolled up and proceeded to unfurl it. There was a great laugh and, to cover it, I said, "Mum, mum, they are laughing at me." I repeated this in a couple of broadcasts, then Brian Sears (the producer) said, "I shouldn't do that line about your mother any more." So I said, "It's my mother's birthday today -can I do it just the once?" The following week I started getting letters saying, "As soon as we hear 'Mum, mum' we know we are in for a good laugh" - so naturally it became my catchphrase!'

my little perforations! 'You have to admit', says Roy Hudd, 'that any business which allows a catchphrase to turn you into a household name, buy you a house in the country and a certain amount of financial security for you and your family, has to be crazy.' He refers to the line from his Quick Brew Tea commercials: 'It's not me, mam, it's me little perforations.' (See also **nice one, Cyril!**)

my name's Friday - I'm a cop! *Dragnet.*

my name's Monica! Beryl Reid as Archie's little friend in *Educating Archie.* Beryl comments: 'Even though I've done so many other things, straight acting parts, and so on, people always remember these little phrases and want me to say them still.'

my name's Sidney Mincing! (See **do you mind!**)

my reply is on a piece of paper! Al Read.

nanu, nanu! salutation from Mork (Robin Williams) of *Mork And Mindy*.

naughty bits! *Monty Python's Flying Circus,* like most graduate comedy shows of the 1960s and '70s, rather frowned upon catchphrases as something more relevant to another type of show business. (But see also **and now for something completely different!** and **wink wink, nudge nudge, say no more!**)

needle, nardle, noo! *The Goon Show.*

negidicrop dibombit! (See **eyaydon, yauden,** etc.)

nice one, Cyril! Originating in a TV commercial for Wonderloaf, in which bakers congratulated each other on their wares, this phrase was taken up by supporters of Spurs footballer Cyril Knowles. They even recorded a song about him with this title. As such, this is one of the most successful - and certainly one of the best - catchphrases to have entered the language from TV advertising.
Barry Day, President of McCann & Co, the advertising agency, comments on the phenomenon in general:
'It occurs to me that *most* of the truly memorable and mind-nagging lines come in the early days of commercial TV - **can you tell Stork from butter?/ you'll wonder where the yellow went when you brush your teeth with Pepsodent!/ you'll be a little lovelier each day with fabulous pink Camay!** - I suspect that's because early TV was very self-consciously a moving version of print advertising, which had always depended very heavily on the slogan or pay-off line. And just about everything was sung. But from the 1960s there was the

revival of the catchphrase type of slogan along the lines of the radio programme ones of the war years. Again, you were consciously trying to create popularity. You *hoped* the comics would take them up and make them part of the language (as opposed to the accidental and usually rude borrowings of slogans like "Can *you* tell Stork . . . ?", etc). Examples of the 'planted' lines would include:
I'm only here for the beer! (Double Diamond)
Are you getting enough? (Milk)
Refreshes the parts other beers cannot reach. (Heineken)
What your right arm's for. (Courage)
'There have also been a number of fortunate accidents - fortunate in that, although the line was intended, its impact was unexpected:
Sccchh - you know who . . . ! (Schweppes)
Full of Eastern Promise. (Fry's Turkish Delight)
Nice one, Cyril! (Wonderloaf)
The Right One. (Martini)
Don't forget the fruit gums, mum. (Rowntree's Fruit Gums)
'It's quite fascinating to re-analyse advertising from this point of view!' (See also **all human life is there!**/ **don't forget the fruit gums, mum!**/ **my little perforations!**/ **roses grow on you!**/ **that'll do nicely, sir!**)

nice to see you, to see you - nice! Greeting, completed by the audience, from Bruce Forsyth in his *Generation Game.*

nick, nick, nick! Jim Davidson providing a vocal counterpart for the revolving light on top of a police vehicle.

nikky, nokky, noo! Nonsense phrase devised by Ken Dodd. 'Humour is anarchic, I suppose,' he says, 'So, like a child, from time to time you revolt against the discipline of words and just jabber!'

ninety-two! Albert Modley in *Variety Bandbox*.

nobody tells me nothing / nobody tells no one nothing! Dan Dungeon, the gloomy scouser, played by Deryck Guyler, in *ITMA*.

no cups outside! Said in an Ulster accent by Ruby Rockcake (Mary O'Farrell) in *ITMA* - reflecting her early upbringing in a railway refreshment room.

no likey? oh crikey? Usually said by Ali Oop (Horace Percival), *ITMA's* saucy post card vendor, who frequently rhymed English idioms like 'very jolly - oh golly!' or 'your hands are grimy - Grimy? Oh blimey!' Peter Black, the former TV critic, once wrote: 'This lunatic exchange sank so deeply into the minds of the girl I was to marry and myself that we still use it thirty years later.'

nookie! A word of innuendo popularised by the ventriloquist Roger de Courcey, who calls his bear 'Nookie'. Hence, 'I like Nookie,' etc.

not a lot! Paul Daniels, the Yorkshire magician and comedian, says he found this catchphrase early on in his career. 'I feel it has done a lot to establish my identity with the public.' In full, it goes: 'You're going to like it . . . not a lot . . . but you'll like it!' - and variations upon the same.

not arf! A verbal mannerism, somewhat

cultivated, of the disc-jockey, Alan
Freeman.

not a word to Bessie! Kenneth Horne,
referring to his fictional wife, in *Much
Binding In The Marsh*.

nothing at all, nothing at all! Signor So-So
(Dino Galvani), an Italian murdering the
English language, in *ITMA*.
Tommy Handley: 'Now, have you anything
to say before I go?'
So-So: 'Notting at all, notting at all!'

not on your Nellie! Eric Partridge dates this
from the late 1930s and says that it is
abbreviated rhyming slang for 'puff
(breath), as in 'not on your Nellie Duff!'
meaning 'not on your life'. Popularised
after the Second World War by Frankie
Howerd.

not so much a . . . more a way of life!
Verbal structure popularised in Britain
from 1964 onwards by the title of the late-
night BBC TV show *Not So Much A
Programme . . . More A Way Of Life*.

not until after six o'clock! The Mayfair Girl
played by Patricia Hayes with an affected
drawl in *Ray's A Laugh*.

not you, momma, siddown! Ben Lyon in
Hi Gang! (Once reported as having
appeared as a piece of graffiti on the
underside of a train lavatory seat.)

now, now, come, come, don't dilly-dally!
Charley Come-Come in *ITMA*.

now there's a beaut if ever there was one! A
failed catchphrase. Bob Monkhouse
remembers: 'As a comedian in the early
1950s, I had one unique aspect. I was
without a catchphrase. Radio producers
sympathised and made suggestions. Charlie
Chester even offered to give me one.
"Every time you score a big laugh, just
remember to dance a little jig and say 'Now
there's a beaut if ever there was one!'" I
politely declined and Charlie, never a comic
to waste material, repeated it in his next
series until it's consistent failure to please
drove him to ad-lib another line, a plea for
audience reponse - "Speak to Charlee-ee!"
- which proved to be a genuine winner.'

now, there's a coincidence! Harold Berens,
the Glasgow-born comedian often believed
to be Cockney, acquired this catchphrase
from a woman who used to sell him his
carnation buttonhole. To everything he said
she replied, 'Now, there's a coincidence!'

now, there's a funny thing! Max Miller.

och man, you're daft! (followed by a laugh 'like a tinkling bell, rippling up the scale') - Molly Weir as Tattie MacKintosh in *ITMA*.

In his book *Sometime Never* Wilfred Pickles gives an eleborate account of how the phrase got into the programme. According to his rather show-biz version, 'Tommy Handley was having a joke at Molly's expense during a break in rehearsal, when she exclaimed, "Och man, you're daft!" Tommy's eyes flashed. He pointed ecstatically at Molly, "We're going to use that!" '

Molly herself says this is fanciful. 'Ted Kavanagh, the writer, simply put it in as a Scots expression.' Indeed, when she subsequently joined *Life With The Lyons* she was kitted out with the inevitable, 'Och, Mr Lyon!'

oh, calamity! Robertson Hare's woeful catchphrase stems from an Aldwych farce of long ago - perhaps when this much put-upon little man had lost his trousers - but even he was unable to remember precisely which one.

oh, get in there, Moreton! Quite the saddest of the catchphrases in this book. Robert Moreton had a brief taste of fame as tutor in *Educating Archie* and was noted for his Bumper Fun Book. After only a year he was dropped from the show, was unable to get other work, and committed suicide.

oh, get on with it! Occasional heckle by Kenneth Williams to fellow cast members in *Beyond Our Ken* and *Round The Horne*.

oh, good show! Terry-Thomas.

oh hello, I'm Julian and this is my friend, Sandy! Spoken by Hugh Paddick referring to Kenneth Williams when they both played a couple of gay ex-chorus boys in *Round The Horne*. They introduced the camp *parlare* (talk) of the *omipalomi* (homosexual) sub culture of actors and dancers to the comfortable drawing-rooms of Radio 4 listeners. *Fantabulosa* (excellent)!

oh, I say, I am a fool! The pay-off line of Dudley Davenport (Maurice Denham) in *Much Binding In The Marsh*. Once advertised as the subject of a sermon by a Methodist minister in Brighton. (Ken Platt uses the shorter, 'oh, I am a fool!')

oh, I say, I rather care for that, hahaha-haa-ha! Flying Officer Kite, the ex-RAF officer, complete with handlebar moustache and varsity accent, played by Humphrey Lestocq in *Merry Go Round*. Lestocq recalls: 'When the show started, I'd just left the RAF. I was madly air-force - "Whacko!", "Good-o!", "Bang on!", all that sort of thing, and this really fascinated Eric Barker. So he went away and found this character for me.' After many a 'wizard prang!', Eric Barker would slap Kite down, but he would only roar 'Oh, I say, I rather care for that' in return. The producer, Leslie Bridgmont, once commented: 'When we introduced the character we worked out this pay-off very carefully . . . the rhythm of the laugh, for instance, had to be exactly the same each time. It is this inexorable sameness that establishes a phrase.'

oh, jolly D! (short for 'jolly decent') Maurice Denham as Dudley Davenport in *Much Binding In The Marsh*.

oh, Mavis! Dick Bentley's poet in *Take It From Here*.

oh, Moses! Derek Nimmo in the TV series *All Gas And Gaiters.* Pauline Devaney and Edwin Apps who wrote it remember: 'Derek was always asking for a catchphrase and we always resisted the suggestion until one day a neighbour who was a pillar of the church, discussing something over the garden wall, said "Moses!" and we wrote it into the script. Derek leapt on it and thereafter used it with such frequency that we eventually got a notice to the effect that it was time the writers stopped putting in "Moses" whenever they couldn't think of anything funny!'

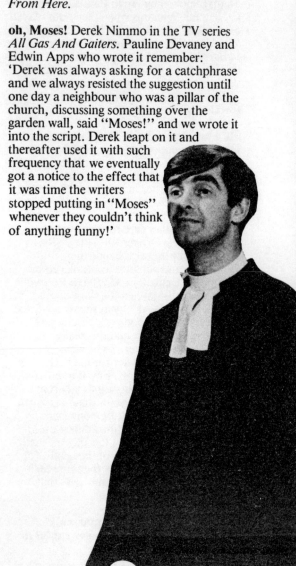

oh, Ron! / yes, Eth? The immortal exchange between June Whitfield as Eth and Dick Bentley as Ron in *Take It From Here* (subsequently reproduced as *The Glums* on TV). A stock phrase rather than a catchphrase, but it became popular because of Eth's rising inflexion and Ron's flat response.

oh, what 'ave I sayed? 'I've always wanted to see Stewart Grainger in the flesh. Oh! what 'ave I sayed?' - Maurice Denham as Ivy Placket in *Much Binding In The Marsh*.

oi! Bud Flanagan's way of rounding off a joke or explanation in his routines with partner, Chesney Allen.

old nasty! A reference to Hitler from *Band Waggon* (nasty/Nazi) - in particular, the edition broadcast on 30 September 1939. (Arthur Askey claims, in similar vein, to have coined the epithet 'Aunty' for the BBC.)

old ones, new ones, loved ones, neglected ones! The pianist Semprini's opening patter.

on behalf of the committee-ee! Colin Crompton as the concert chairman of ITV's *Wheeltappers And Shunters Social Club*. Colin says: 'Letters by the score told me my catchphrases were a schoolteachers' nightmare. And we had so many children outside the house, shouting them out, that we were forced to move to a quieter neighbourhood! Although it is several years since the last programme was transmitted, the phrases have remained popular and I'm flattered that most impressionists include them in their acts.'

on behalf of the working classes! Music-hall comedian Billy Russell (1893-1971).

only in the mating season! *The Goon Show's* traditional response to the chatting-up line, 'Do you come here often?'

ooh, an' 'e was strong! Al Read.

ooh, Betty! A key phrase for impersonators of Frank Spencer, Michael Crawford's character in *Some Mothers Do Have 'Em*.

ooh, bold! very bold! Julian and/or Sandy in *Round The Horne*.

ooh, I say! (what a dream volleh!) Dan Maskell's voice in his Wimbledon commentaries is as much part of the atmosphere surrounding tennis as Peter O'Sullevan's is redolent of hot leather, perspiring horses and binoculars at race meetings.

ooh, mother! George Formby's characteristic cry, scurrying away from trouble.

ooh, you are awful - but I like you! Dick Emery as Mandy - the last word is followed by a quick bash with her handbag. The title of a song and a feature film.

open the box! Contestants in the old ITV quiz *Take Your Pick* were given the option of opening a numbered box (which might contain anything from tickets for a holiday to Ena Sharples's hairnet) or 'taking the money'. The studio audience would chant their advice to hesitating contestants. When the host, Michael Miles, died, it was said that his funeral had been interrupted by the congregation shouting, 'Open the box! Open the box!' The show ran for almost twenty years from 1955.

open the door, Richard! A line from a song first sung in Britain on *ITMA*.

orft we jolly well go! One of a number of verbal tricks performed regularly by Jimmy Young after his switch from singing to radio deejaying. Note also his frequent recourse to the phrases 'You see!' and 'I ask myself'.

ours is a nice 'ouse ours is! Cyril Fletcher.

'ow do, 'ow are yer? 'Ladies and gentlemen of Bingley, 'ow do, 'ow are yer?' - that is how Wilfred Pickles introduced the first edition of *Have A Go* in 1946. (Alternatively ' 'ow are yer? all right?') Within a year the show had an audience of 20 million and ran for twenty-one years. Pickles died in 1978.

qué?

pardon? Almost raised to catchphrase status by Eric Morecambe.

pass! From *The Times* (8 November 1977): 'For proof of how Magnus Magnusson's television programme *Mastermind* is catching on, I would refer to you this story sent in by a reader from London NW6. He was accosted by a small lad, asking for a penny for the guy. On being asked if he knew who Guy Fawkes was, the lad replied with engaging honesty: "Pass." '

permission to speak, sir! Lance-Corporal Jones (Clive Dunn) in TV's *Dad's Army*.

pin back your lugholes!
Cyril Fletcher's customary cry before embarking upon one of his Odd Odes.

play it again, Sam! As is now well known, nowhere in the film *Casablanca* does Humphrey Bogart say this phrase. At one point Ingrid Bergman says, 'Play it once, Sam, for old time's sake', and later on Bogart says, 'You played it for her, you can play it for me. Play it!' But, what the hell -the phrase exists!

play the game, cads! The Western Brothers (who were, in fact, cousins) would begin their act with 'Hello, cads!' and end it with, 'Cheerio, cads, and happy landings!'

play the music and open the cage! Arthur English in his spiv persona. He recalls: 'During my first show at the Windmill I finished up my act halfway through a joke, looking at the front row and saying, "You'll be here next house - I'll tell you the end then!" But when I was asked to do a further six-week season at the "Mill", I thought, "I can't do the same ending" and as I can't sing all that well I was stuck for a finish. I started rambling on with the senseless chatter I became known for and my wife, Joy, said, "That's funny - finish with that." So I did and got to the end of my act and suddenly realised I had no finish to the chatter! I don't know what made me say it, but I said, "I don't know what the devil I'm talking about. Play the music. Open the cage!" and ran off.'

please yourselves! Frankie Howerd. Used as the title of a radio series.

poor soul - she's past it! Was said by Frankie Howerd of his supposedly deaf accompanist - alternatively, 'poor old thing - she'll have to go!'

possums! Term of endearment used by Dame Edna Everage (Barry Humphries).

Priscilla, she's my best friend and I hate her! Monica (Beryl Reid) in *Educating Archie*.

proper Charlie! Charlie Chester. Used by him as the title of a radio show.

proper humdrum! *Band Waggon*.

proper poorly! 'I didn't feel well, I didn't. I felt poorly - proper poorly!' Reg Dixon, famous for his 'Confidentially' theme tune.

¿qué? Manuel the Spanish waiter (played by Andrew Sachs) in *Fawlty Towers*.

quick thinking, Batman! Typically crawling remark from sidekick, Robin.

Ramsbottom, Enoch and me!

Ramsbottom, Enoch and me! Radio's
Happidrome was ruled by Harry Korris as
Mr Lovejoy, a theatre manager, Cecil
Fredericks as Ramsbotton, and Robby
Vincent as Enoch, the call-boy. This phrase
was part of the introductory song.

**Ray, Ray, step into my office a minute,
Ray!** Laidman Browne as Mr Tumble in
Ray's A Laugh, circa 1960.

read any good books lately? Richard
Murdoch's way of changing the subject in
Much Binding In The Marsh:
Horne: One of the nicest sandwiches I've
ever had. What was it, Murdoch?
Murdoch: Well, there was - er - have you
read any good books lately?
Horne: I thought it tasted something like
that.
An old phrase, of course. Also used in
Band Waggon, and air-force *Merry Go
Round.*

rhubarb! The heroic cry, further
popularised by *The Goon Show.*

right monkey! 'She said, "Did he say
anything about the check suit?" and I
thought, "Right monkey!"' - Al Read.
Gerry Collins of Manchester's Music Hall
Association adds: 'My mother used to say
this to me *years* before Al Read's pro-time.
When I refused to go an errand because I
was busy playing, she'd say, "Right,
monkey, wait till your father comes home"
- which shows how talented Al Read was,
to store up in his mind all these real
Lancashire gems and, in after years, be able
to reproduce them.' From a theatre poster
seen in Blackpool: 'HENRY HALL
PRESENTS AL READ IN "RIGHT
MONKEY"' (See also **cheeky monkey!**)

rock on, Tommy! Bobby Ball to Tommy Cannon (Cannon and Ball).

roses grow on you! An advertising slogan for Cadbury's Roses chocolates. Norman Vaughan says: 'This was shouted at me wherever I went from about 1965. It was based on a TV advert of which I made only eight and the campaign only ran for two years. But on personal appearances even now people still ask me, "Where are your roses?"!' (See also **nice one, Cyril!**)

sapristi! (as in 'sapristi nuckoes', etc) Spike Milligan as Count Jim Moriarty in *The Goon Show*.

say goodnight, Dick / Goodnight, Dick! Rowan to Martin in *Laugh-In,* echoing George Burns and Gracie Allen.
Burns: Say goodnight, Gracie.
Allen: Goodnight, Gracie!

say no more! (See wink wink, nudge, nudge, say no more!)

see you later, alligator! (in a while, crocodile) From the title of a Bill Haley hit in the film *Rock Around The Clock*.

seriously, though, he's doing a grand job! Would-be conciliation by David Frost after any satirical attack on *That Was The Week That Was,* 1962-63. I can remember it being seized on by clergymen and others but Ned Sherrin, the producer, claims that the phrase was used no more than half a dozen times altogether on the show.

serve that lady with a crusty loaf! Arthur Askey on *Band Waggon*. 'Why I said that, I've no idea. It came from out of the blue when some woman was laughing very loud in the studio audience. Perhaps it goes back to the days when I used to do the shopping for my mum in Liverpool and I picked it up then.'

settle down now, settle down! Ken Goodwin attempting to quieten laughter at his own jokes: 'Settle down, now . . . I don't want you to make a noise, I've got a headache.' A catchphrase cleverly based on the observation that if you tell people not to laugh they will only do so the more (cf. George Robey's **desist!**).

Ken recalls: 'I first said "Settle down" in a working men's club after the so-called compère/chairman had announced me to the audience. They didn't hear him and they didn't know I was on stage till I let them know. They were so noisy that, to get attention, I said, "Come on, you lot, settle down now." One or two began to smile and say to themselves, "What's this unknown commodity?" They were all waiting for bingo! It really took off after doing the Royal Variety Show, a summer season at the Palladium and *The Comedians.*'

sharpen up there, the quick stuff's coming! A necessary exhortation to audiences from Arthur English in his late 1940s spiv character who used to spiel at some three hundred words a minute. But Arthur says: 'It didn't really get off the ground. One of my scriptwriters put it in - but strangely enough it was the catchphrases we didn't plan that caught on.'

she knows, you know! Diminutive comedienne, Hylda Baker, about her mute giraffe-like butt, Cynthia.

she seems like a nice girl, doesn't she? Larry Grayson in *The Generation Game,* which he took over from Bruce Forsyth in 1978.

she's only eight! Max Bygraves in radio's *Paradise Street, circa* 1954.

short, fat, hairy legs! Applied to Ernie Wise by Eric Morecambe in contrast to his own long, elegant legs. Ernie says that this emerged, like most of their catchphrases, during rehearsals - particularly during their spell with ATV.

show us your rabbit! Inspired phrase used in (Raymond) Bennett and (Harry) Moreny's variety act.

shut that door! Larry Grayson, fending off rheumatism again.
Larry Grayson's rapid rise to fame in the early 1970s stemmed from a four minute TV spot he was offered out of the blue. This was the first time he used the phrase 'shut that door!' He said, 'It's so draughty in here. I've got my surgical stocking on and it's not working!' Within a year he was in the cast of the Royal Variety Show.

shut your mouth, Soppy! Said by, or about, a character called Soppy (Peter Sellers) in *Ray's A Laugh*.

silly old moo! Alf Garnett (Warren Mitchell) to his wife (Dandy Nichols) in *Till Death Us Do Part* - a euphemism for cow, but Dandy Nichols says people used to call it out to her in the street affectionately.

sir, I have an idea! ('You haven't, Murdoch' - 'Yes, I have . . .') Richard Murdoch and Kenneth Horne in *Much Binding In The Marsh.*

(the) sixty-four thousand dollar question 'Ah, that's the sixty-four dollar question, isn't it?' people will exclaim, when surely they mean 'sixty-four *thousand* dollar question'? Well, put it down to inflation: *Webster's Dictionary* says that $64 *was* the highest award in a CBS radio quiz called *Take It Or Leave It* which ran from 1941 to 1948. That was how the phrase entered common parlance but subsequently the money for the highest prize in the quiz was raised to $64,000. When ITV imported the show it was called simply *The 64,000 Question,* cleverly making no mention of dollars or pounds.

(the) size of it! Alex Munro, Scots entertainer.

smashin! Expression used by Bernard Bresslaw as the gormless Bernard of *Educating Archie.*

smile, please - watch the birdie! *ITMA,* from the traditional photographer's instructions.

'sno use! Harry Weldon (1881-1930), the 's' pronounced with a loud whistle. From the title of a song.

sock it to me! This provided *Laugh-In* with its basic, much-repeated gag. The English actress Judy Carne would chant 'sock it to me!' over and over until - endlessly unsuspecting - she would be drenched in water or clubbed. The phrase 'to sock it to someone' has been traced back to Mark Twain via Negro jazz. A sexual meaning is, of course, implicit.

somebody come! Jimmy James in his 'drunk' bedroom sketch.

somebody pinched me puddin! Variety act Collinson and Breen.

soopersonic! Eddie Large's catchword for Syd Little (Little and Large).

sorree! Little and Large.

speak as you find, that's my motto! This was the catchphrase of Nola, the stubbornly unmarried daughter of Mrs

Purvis, the studio cleaner, in Arthur Askey's radio show *Hello Playmates!* Bob Monkhouse (who wrote it with Denis Goodwin) called them 'a truly marvellous pair of characters who sprang into life fully-blossomed in our first script for the show. They were played by Irene Handl as the mother, forever foisting her undesirable offspring on every male as a perfect bride, and Pat Coombs as the curiously self-composed Nola, whose smug excuse for the appalling insults she hurled was, "Well . . . speak as you find, that's my motto." '

In 1955 *Hello Playmates!* won the *Daily Mail* Radio Award for the year's top show and this catchphrase was inscribed on the presentation silver microphone - which was rather odd considering that the show's star, Arthur Askey, had never uttered it.

steady, Barker! This was employed in Eric Barker's radio series *Merry Go Round* and *Just Fancy.* In his autobiography, *Steady Barker,* published in 1956, Barker recalled that the phrase arose by chance one day and immediately caught on. 'It could be used on so many occasions . . . it almost passed into the language. Also each time it was quoted it gave me the all-vital personal publicity . . . I have had letters from those who have said it helped them to cure a lifelong habit of swearing, as they were able to use it instead. One old lady who shared a flat with an awkward sister at Cheltenham said they had been in danger of drifting apart, but that now, lo! when they reached a point when it seemed neither could endure the bickering a moment longer, they both said, "Steady Barker!" and it cleared the air. I also learned it was sent as a naval signal from a C-in-C to a ship whose gunfire was a little wide of the mark.'

stop! (See **carry on, London!**)

stop it, you sauce box! Crystal Jellybottom, a charlady played by Patricia Hayes in *Ray's A Laugh*.

stop messing about! Kenneth Williams in his nudging voice. The phrase started when he was a supporting actor in *Hancock's Half Hour*. Later the title of a radio series in which he starred. Ray Galton says of the start of *Hancock* in 1954: 'Alan Simpson and I wanted a show without breaks, guest singers and catchphrases - something that hadn't been done before. After the first week with Kenneth in the show, bang went our ideas of no funny voices and no catchphrases!'

(boss, boss) sumpin' terrible's happened!
Sam Scram (Sydney Keith), Tommy
Handley's American henchman in *ITMA*.
Spoken in a gangster-like drawl.

surely . . ! Characteristic interjection by
Julian Huxley in *The Brains Trust*.

sur le telephoneo! Said by Jimmy Young,
who established himself as a radio
personality, first by chatting to housewives
on the phone, second by taking his show on
a tour of European capitals to mark
Britain's entry into the EEC, hence **'sur le
continong'** (See also **what's the recipe
today?**)

swingin'! (accompanied by a thumbs up gesture) Norman Vaughan of the swinging sixties. Norman recalls: ' "Swinging'!" and "Dodgy!" came originally from my association with jazz musicians and just seemed to creep into my everyday conversation. Then when I got the big break at the Palladium they were the first catchphrases that the papers and then the public seized upon. According to *The Making Of The Prime Minister, 1964,* by Anthony Howard and Richard West, "Swingin'!" was the basis of the advertising campaign for the Labour Party from January 1963!'

take 'im away, Ramsbottom! *Happidrome.*

tatty-bye! Ken Dodd inherited this farewell from his dad.

taxi! *ITMA.*

tea, Gregory/Edmund? Hermione Gingold, radio *Grande Gingold, circa* 1955.

terrific! (pronounced 'terr-if-ic!') Mike Reid, the cockney comedian. (See also **it's terrific!**)

thanking you! Cyril Fletcher (pronounced 'thenking yew').

that'll do nicely, sir! Crawling acquiescence to offer of American Express card in TV commercial for same. (See also **nice one, Cyril!**)

that's tantamount to a rebuff! *Band Waggon.*

that's the boy! *ITMA.*

that's the way it is, folks! Walter Cronkite, at the end of CBS TV news broadcasts.

that's yer lot! (See **aye, aye, that's yer lot!**)

that's your actual French! Julian and Sandy first appeared in *Round The Horne* in April 1964. One of their incarnations was as film producers:
Sandy: Mr Horne, we are in the forefront of your *Nouvelle Vague.* That's your actual French.
Julian: It means we are of the New Wave.
Sandy: And very nice it looks on you, too.
(See also **oh hello, I'm Julian . . .** and **ooh, bold . . .**) (Peter Cook claims to have

launched 'your actual' as a turn of phrase).

that was a good one, was it not? Jimmy Edwards, commending one of his own jokes on *Take It From Here*.

that was not very tasteful! Lily Tomlin in *Laugh-In*.

them's the conditions that prevail! Jimmy 'Schnozzle' Durante.

there'll never be another! ('Miller's the name, lidy. There'll never . . .') Max Miller.

there's no answer to that! Eric Morecambe's standard innuendo-laden response to such comments as:
Frank Finlay (as Casanova): I'll be perfectly frank with you - I have a long felt want.

there we are, dear friends, both home, overseas and over the borders! Charlie Chester's pay-off in his more recent role as a radio presenter. He remembers how it started in about 1970: 'If you say something on the radio you don't know what the reaction's going to be but the boomerang comes back at you. I just wanted to say "goodbye" to everybody listening. At that time on Radio 2 we covered a great deal of the globe and I used to sign off, "There we are, my friends, both home, overseas and over the border." A woman wrote to me from Sweden and said, "Thank you for saying that - I married a Swedish gentleman and I haven't been home since and it makes me feel quite at home to think that you remembered us overseas." So, of course, I kept it in proudly. And eventually I got a letter from a woman saying, "Why do you say 'over the border'? I mean we're in Wales as well as Scotland, you know." So I have to say "borders" now just to embrace everybody.'

(ah,) there you are! *ITMA*.

these are the jokes, folks! Norman Vaughan says: 'On *The Golden Shot* from 1971 for eighteen months I developed this catchphrase because often the studio audience - perhaps overawed by the occasion - would sit in silence as we cracked a few funnies. Either that or the jokes weren't very good! The first time I used the line every joke after it got a laugh. It was later used by two other "name" comics.'

these sets take a long time to warm up! Kenneth Horne in *Much Binding In The Marsh* - indeed they did in the days before the valve was replaced by the transistor.

they're working well tonight! 'Monsewer' Eddie Gray of the Crazy Gang.

thingmy ringmy! Stanley Baxter as Bella in *It's All Yours* - Scottish radio series, *circa* 1953.

thirty-five years! Kenneth Williams as an old man in *Beyond Our Ken*.

this boy's a fool! Eric Morecambe of Ernie Wise.

this is Funf speaking! Spoken sideways into a glass tumbler by Jack Train in *ITMA,* this phrase was 'the embodiment of the nation's spy neurosis' (according to the producer, Francis Worsley). The first time Funf appeared was in the second edition of the programme on 26 September 1939, just after the outbreak of war. Initially, he said, 'Dees ees Foonf, your favourite shpy!' Jack Train recalled that, when Worsley was searching for a good name to call the spy, he overheard his six-year-old son, Roger, trying to count in German: 'Ein, zwei, drei, vier, fünf' - and that's where he always got stuck. Train himself had been to see Akim Tamiroff in a film and was doing impersonations of him in a pub when Worsley came over and said, 'I want you for the spy.' Train spoke into a beer glass and Worsley decided Funf must be on the telephone.

Funf always uttered threats of dire disasters, at which Tommy Handley would laugh - just as the nation subsequently did at the broadcast snidery of Lord Haw-haw. For a while it became a craze always to start phone conversations with the words.

this is Henry Hall speaking! ('and tonight is my guest night') What is the reason for the peculiar emphasis on 'is'? In 1934, the BBC Dance Orchestra had been playing while he was away in America yet it was announced as 'directed by Henry Hall'. A journalist wrote, 'Why do the BBC allow this to happen? How can Henry Hall possibly be conducting the orchestra when we know for a fact that at this very moment he is on the high seas?' Hence, on his return, Hall said, 'Hello everyone, this *is* Henry Hall speaking!'

this is it! (followed by **makes you think!**)
Ritual exchange of views by pub bores
discussing the week's news (played by
David Jason and Bill Wallis) in radio's
Week Ending . . . (Since about 1977).

this is London! Salutation familiar to
American listeners to wartime news given
by Ed Murrow, chief of CBS's foreign
staff. Also used by BBC announcers, of
course. Stuart Hibberd used the phrase as
the title of a book of his broadcasting
diaries.

**this play what
I have wrote!**
Ernie Wise.

this week's deliberate mistake! In an early
broadcast of the 1930s radio series *Monday
Night At Seven* (later *Eight*), Harry S.
Pepper committed some ghastly mistake.
Listeners immediately rang in and Pepper
cleverly extracted himself from the situation
by saying at the end of the show, 'I wonder

how many of you were clever enough to spot my deliberate mistake?'

There was a genuine 'deliberate mistake' every week thereafter and the phrase has entered the language to some extent as a cover for ineptitude.

time for your OBE, Neddie! Captain Grytpype-Thynne (Peter Sellers) to Neddie Seagoon (Harry Secombe) in *The Goon Show*.

to boldly go where no man has gone before! From the introduction to *Star Trek* (the TV film series about split infinity).

(a) touch of the _____! Norman Vaughan introduced this formula during his TV Palladium stint ('A touch of the Nelson Riddles', etc). Later he had a TV series called *A Touch Of The Norman Vaughans*.

(a) tree fell on him! Spike Milligan's running gag from one of his *Q* series on BBC 2.
Q. Are you Jewish?
A. No, a tree fell on me.

TTFN! ('ta-ta for now') The last word of *ITMA's* Mrs Mopp (Dorothy Summers) after having presented the Mayor (Tommy Handley) with his gift ('I brought this for you . . .'). Sometimes the last thing people said before they died in hospital during the war. Still heard today.

'ullo cock! 'ow's yerself? Said in the distinctive gravelly voice of Richard Gray as Baron Waterlogged of Waterlogged Spa in *Merry Go Round*.

ullo, ullo, ullo, what's this? Jimmy Edwards as Pa Glum in *Take It From Here* (usually interrupting his son Ron who was after a kiss from fiancée Eth). Frank Muir says, 'It was not meant to be a catchphrase but as Pa Glum always said it on his entrance - and it was so useful a phrase in everyday life — it caught on.' It also echoes the traditional inquiry of a policeman.

up and down the railway lines! Jack Warner had a monologue on radio's *Monday Night At Eight* about a wheeltapper who won the pools and still referred to his old calling in a mixed cockney and Mayfair drawl - something like 'hup hand dahn the rawlaway lanes'.

up and under! Rugby League term now a standard component in the Eddie Waring impersonator's kit.

veree good sir! Private Warner (Jack Warner) in *Garrison Theatre,* based on producer Harry S. Pepper's memories of such a theatre in the First World War. From the same show, **di-da-di-da** and **a riil mill.**

very interesting . . . but stupid! (pronounced *verry* and with a thick German accent) Arte Johnson as the German soldier in *Laugh-In*.

very tasty, very sweet! Kenway and Young (Nan Kenway and Douglas Young, variety stars) in the radio series *Howdy Folks,* etc.

vicky verky! Said by Fred Yule as Norman in *ITMA*. 'High time you was here, sir. They're fair frantic - or vicky verky!'

vous pouvez cracher! *ITMA* did a skit on pre-war Radio Luxembourg and called it 'Radio Fakenburg'. 'Ici Radio Fakenburg,' the announcer would say. 'Mesdames et messieurs, défense de cracher (no spitting).' Each espisode would end: 'Mesdames et messieurs, vous pouvez cracher!'

wait till I tell the boys! Character with no name in *ITMA*.

wake up at the back there! Jimmy Edwards in *Take It From Here*. Frank Muir comments: 'This was a line I always used in writing Jim's schoolmaster acts. It was technically very useful in breaking up his first line and getting audience attention.' Bob Monkhouse adds: 'Jimmy Edwards's roaring admonition "Wake up at the back there!" had everything I felt a gild-edged catchphrase should have. It was perfectly in character and it arose naturally from Jimmy's actual wrath with a sullen audience. It was short, funny in any setting and *useful* - the kind of all-purpose joke-saving line beloved of comedians who hate to hear a subtle gag go down in silence.' Jim: They laughed at Suez but he went right ahead and built his canal - wake up at the back there!

wakey-wakey! Billy Cotton's *Band Show* ran on radio and TV for over twenty years. For one seven-year period it was broadcast on radio without a break for fifty-two weeks a year. First would come a fanfare, then the call 'Wakey-wakey!' (without the 'rise and shine'), and this was followed by a noisy, brisk rendering of 'Somebody Stole My Gal'. The programme was first broadcast on 6 February 1949 at 10.30 a.m. Because of this, rehearsals had to begin at 8.45 - not the best time to enthuse a band which had just spent six days on the road. 'Oi, come on,' said Cotton, 'Wakey-wakey!' It worked and eventually resulted in such a cheerful atmosphere that the producer said the show might well start with it. 'I thought of all those people lying in their beds,' said Cotton, 'and I remembered the sergeant who used to kick my bottom when I was a kid - and out came the catchword.' Cotton died in 1969, aged sixty-nine.

wave your gladdies! Dame Edna Everage (Barry Humphries). (Well, I think it ought to be a catchphrase.)

we be doomed, we all be doomed! Spasm (Kenneth Williams), Lady Counterblast's butler in *Round The Horne* (perhaps echoing a John Laurie character who would exclaim, 'Doomed I am, doomed'). Barry Took, who wrote the show with Marty Feldman, declares: 'Marty and I went all out to avoid catchphrases but the cast kept pencilling them in. Eventually we gave up the unequal struggle!'

we did it once at Bannockburn! Alec Finlay often portrayed an old Scots Home Guard sergeant. If doubts were expressed about his company's ability, he would reply: 'Dinna worry - we did it once at Bannockburn, we can do the same again!'

we have ways of making you talk! The caricature Gestapo threat (spoken in a thick German accent) revived by *Laugh-In* and other shows.

we'll be back in a trice! Stock phrase of David Frost's, as a variation on 'we'll be right back after this (commercial) break'.

well, for evermore! *ITMA*.

well, ring my chimes! *Rowan And Martin's Laugh-In*.

we've got a right one 'ere! Dick Emery as Mr Monty in *Educating Archie*. (Also employed by Bruce Forsyth, Tony Hancock and Frankie Howerd.)

what a beautiful day for ——! Another example of a Ken Dodd catchphrase which allows for variety by the addition of a joke.

what about Rovers? Failed catchphrase from *Ray's A Laugh,* 1950, according to Ted Ray. 'Unlucky? - what about Rovers?' 'Unlucky? - you don't know you're born!'

what a carry on! Jimmy Jewel, of Jewel and Warris. He would refer to Ben Warris as 'Harry Boy' (for reasons lost in the mists of time) - 'Go on, Harry Boy! Tell 'em, boy. Has Harry Boy been up to something naughty?'

what a common boy! *ITMA.*

what a funny woman! Frankie Howerd describes this and other of his catchphrases as 'verbal punctuation marks'. 'While other shows used catchphrases almost as characters, I was a character who used catchphrases,' he says.

what a gay day! Larry Grayson.

what a ghastly name! Jimmy Edwards in *Take It From Here.* Frank Muir comments: 'A useful (albeit meaningless) line which could always be given to Jimmy when somebody else mentioned a name. In fact I suppose it was quite a funny, deflating way to react.'

what a performance! Sid Field, the comedian (died 1950).

(ee,) what a to-do! Robb Wilton.

what did Horace say? Harry Hemsley, the ventriloquist, whose doll was a small child who always spoke gibberish.

what does it matter what you do as long as you tear 'em up? In *Mediterranean Merry Go Round,* Jon Pertwee played a Devonshire bugler at Plymouth Barracks who eventually became the postman in *Waterlogged Spa* (not to mention thirteenth trombonist in the Spa Symphony Orchestra). At one concert he became bored with the slow movement of a symphony and broke into 'Tiger Rag'. When Eric Barker remonstrated with him, he said: 'Ah, me old darling, but it tore 'em through, didn't it?' Barker: 'Well, er, yes . . . .' Postman: 'Well, what's it matter what you do as long as you tear 'em up?'

what do you think of the show so far? -Rubbish! Eric Morecambe's customary inquiry of audiences animate or inanimate.

what is ———, Papa? 'What *is* kissing, Papa?' - Naive, in *ITMA*.

what me? - in my state of health? Charles Atlas (Fred Yule) in *ITMA*.

what's the recipe today, Jim? Jimmy Young's recipe spot on his radio show is heralded not only by a jingle extolling the merits of 'home cooking' but also by the chipmunk-voiced Raymondo making this inquiry. Jim recites the ingredients for Cabbage and Custard Surprise, or some such delicacy, then Raymondo intones, 'And this is what you do!'

what's up, Doc? The characteristic inquiry of Bugs Bunny, the cartoon character -phrase subsequently used as the title of a film starring Barbra Streisand and Ryan O'Neal.

what was the question? Goldie Hawn, in *Laugh-In*.

whatwhatwhatwhat! Harry Secombe as Seagoon in *The Goon Show.*

what would you do, chums? A regular feature of *Band Waggon* was a tale told by the actor, Syd Walker, in the character of a junkman. He would pose some everyday dilemma and end with the query or some variation upon it, such as, 'Well, what do you *think,* chums?' Walker died during the Second World War.

what your right arm's for! (See **nice one, Cyril!**)

when I'm dead and gone, the game's finished! Max Miller.

when I was in Patagonia . . . ! Commander A B Campbell was one of the regulars on BBC radio's *Brains Trust,* but it was on an earlier version of the programme, called *Any Questions,* that he came up with his famous phrase. Donald McCullough, the chairman, said: 'Mr Edwards of Balham wants to know if the members of the Brains Trust agree with the practice of sending missionaries to foreign lands.'
C E M Joad and Julian Huxley gave their answers and then Campbell began, 'Well, when I was in Patagonia . . .'
In a book which used the phrase as its title, Campbell recalled: 'I got no further, for Joad burst into a roar of laughter and the other members of the session joined in. For some time the feature was held up while the hilarity spent itself. For the life of me I could not see the joke . . . I got hundreds of letters and it cost me a small fortune in stamps . . . Even today (1951), years after, I can raise a laugh if I am on a public platform and make an illusion to it.'

where did you get that hat? A catchphrase of the 1890s, originating in a comic song of J J Sullivan.

where did you learn to kiss like that? Bob Monkhouse: 'In my script-writing partnership with Denis Goodwin I must confess to the deliberate confecting of catchphrases. From our first major radio success, *Calling All Forces,* came 'Where did you learn to kiss like that?' But it was what we called a ''vehicle phrase'', not really constructed to catch on but to carry a fresh joke each week! (*Calling All Forces* was first broadcast on 3 December 1950.)

where's me shirt? 'Like most performers,' says Ken Dodd, 'I'm always trying out material on friends and relatives. One night after recording my radio show in London, we rushed to catch the train back to Knotty Ash from Euston. I was trying on various daft voices and saying, ''Where's me case? Where's me shirt?'' and the people who were with me laughed - so it went in the next show!' The pronunciation is approximately, 'whairs me shairt?' Also, **I'm a shairt short!**

where've you been, who've you been with, what've you been doing, and why? Old Mother Riley, to her daughter. (See also **Mrs Ginocchi, SOS!**)

Whippit Kwick! This was actually the name of a cat-burglar in Charlie Chester's *Stand Easy* - a character in a radio strip cartoon. Charlie remembers how the name came to him: 'I was standing in Park Lane and a newspaper placard said ''FUR COAT ROBBERIES'' and I thought of a Persian cat-burglar. But I knew nothing about Persian cats, so that limited it. Then I thought the opposite of "cat" is "dog" -how about a whippet? "Whip it" means "to steal it", so "Whippit Kwick"! We did that as a repetition joke and it became a catchphrase.'

Leslie Bridgmont, producer of the show, recalled how the name swept the country. Wherever he went, he said, on bus, tube or train, he would hear someone say, 'Who's that over there?' to which would come the reply, 'Whippit Kwick'.

Charlie Chester adds: 'Everybody knew the phrase. Bruce Woodcock, the boxer, used to run around the streets chanting the jungle chants from the same strip cartoon, "Down in the jungle, living in a tent, better than a pre-fab - no rent", that sort of thing. Once he was fighting at Wembley and I was invited as his guest. Just before he threw a right to put the other fellow out for the count, some wag in the audience yelled out, "Whippit Kwick!" He did -and it went in. That was the end of the fight and the phrase couldn't have come at a better time.'

who loves ya, baby?
Telly Savalas, as the lollipop-sucking New York police lieutenant in *Kojak*.

wink wink, nudge nudge, say no more! Eric Idle's prurient character in *Monty Python's Flying Circus.* 'Is your wife a goer then? Eh? Eh?'

(ee,) wot a geezer! Harold Berens, who became known through the post-war radio show *Ignorance Is Bliss,* used to live near the Bayswater Road in London. He would buy his daily newspaper there from a vendor who always asked him, 'Wot's the latest joke?' When told, this was his customary reaction.

wotcher mates! Danny La Rue attempting to reassure us that all is not lost.

would you Adam-and-Eve it! A touch of rhyming slang from Mildred (Norma Ronald) in radio's long-running series based on the Civil Service, *The Men From The Ministry.* Edward Taylor, whose brainchild it was, says: 'We didn't think in terms of catchphrases but I could think of fifty times each, for example, when Deryck Guyler said, "Ugly business!" or Richard Murdoch, "The mind boggles!" '

wu-hey! For his character of Alf Ippititimus, Jack Douglas has created what, for me, is one of the most compelling visual and verbal catchphrases of all. The bodily twitch which accompanies this cry defies description. The combination was born when Jack was appearing in a double act with Joe Baker at a holiday camp many years ago. Joe managed to get himself locked out of the theatre and Jack found himself alone on the stage. 'My mind went completely bank and in sheer desperation I began twitching and falling about.'

yackabakaka! Count Jim Moriarty (Spike Milligan) in *The Goon Show* - as in 'Stopppp! Ferma yackabakaka le Pune!'

ying-tong-iddle-i-po! All-purpose phrase from *The Goon Show* - most notably incorporated in 'The Ying Tong Song'.

you ain't heard nothin' yet (folks)! Ad-lib remark by Al Jolson in *The Jazz Singer,* the first full-length talking picture, released in New York, October 1927.

you bet your sweet bippy! Dick Martin (usually) in *Rowan and Martin's Laugh-In.*

you can't get the wood, you know! Minnie Bannister or Henry Crun in *The Goon Show.*

you can't see the join! Eric Morecambe to Ernie Wise of his (presumed) hair-piece. Ernie says:. 'We once shared digs in Chiswick with an American acrobat who had a toupee which - like all toupees - was perfectly obvious as such. We would whisper to each other, out of the side of our mouths, "You can hardly see the join!"'

you dirty old man! The younger Steptoe (Harry H. Corbett) to his father, in *Steptoe And Son.*

you dirty rat! James Cagney claims he never said the words put in his mouth by countless impressionists. In *Blonde Crazy,* however, he does call someone a 'dirty, double-crossing rat' - which, I suppose, amounts to much the same thing.

you (dirty) rotten swine, you! Bluebottle (Peter Sellers) in *The Goon Show.* Also, **you have deaded me!**

you gotta go oww! Moriarty (Spike Milligan) in *The Goon Show.*

you'll be lucky I say, you'll be lucky! Al Read.

you lucky people! Tommy Trinder rode on a wave of publicity in the early 1940s. Advertising hoardings declared, 'If it's laughter you're after, Trinder's the name. You lucky people!' Used as the title of a film in 1954. The phrase (which arose in concert party) led to what Charlie Chester describes as 'one of the fastest ad-libs in the history of showbusiness': 'Trinder was working at a London club and was just coming up as the young man with the very quick brain and the very quick ad-libs. He used to give his photographs out and walk round the tables in a hurried manner saying, "Trinder's the name, you lucky people!" So he walked towards Orson Welles, who'd just had a divorce from Rita Hayworth, and said, "Trinder's the name", giving him a photograph. Orson Welles, sprawled out with his legs apart, said very aggressively, "Why don't you change it?" Quick as a flash, Trinder said, "Are you proposing?" And Orson Welles sank like a pricked balloon!'

you're far too wee! Dave Willis, Scots entertainer.

you're the kind of people who give me a bad name! Max Miller.

you shouldn't have done that! Robb Wilton as Mr Muddlecombe to Lauri Lupino Lane as Adolphus.

you should use stronger elastic! From the first major radio series for the troops after the Second World War, *Calling All Forces*. Ted Ray was the star host and Bob Monkhouse and Denis Goodwin, former Dulwich College boys, teamed up to script the comedy sequences. In the first show, broadcast live at noon on Sunday 3 December 1950, the guests were Jimmy Edwards, Jean Kent, then a major British film star, and Freddie Mills, the world light-heavyweight champion. Mills, departing from his script, told of one punch he received when he lowered his gloves. He added, quite seriously, 'My trainer nearly fainted when he saw me drop 'em. I didn't mean to drop 'em.' Ted Ray heard a ripple of laughter as the audience perceived a double meaning and immediately responded, 'You should use stronger elastic.' The roar of laughter this line provoked sent Monkhouse and Goodwin hurrying backstage to augment the script for a Napoleon and Josephine sketch. They gave Jean Kent an extra line - 'I have only flimsy defences against your passionate advance and I can't even keep them up!' -so that Ted Ray, as Napoleon, could repeat his ad-lib line from the Mills interview. This he did. The laughter and applause stopped the show for a full minute and the two young writers, aged twenty-one, were severely reprimanded by the Director of Variety, for circumventing the censor.

By mid-week, however, the phrase had

caught on. A cartoon appeared in the *Daily Sketch* depicting Clement Attlee in drag, tripped up by a pair of bloomers around his ankles bearing the unlikely phrase, 'The National Health Act', while a chirpy Winston Churchill leaned out of a Broadcasting House window and called out, 'Caught you with your plans down, Clem! You should use stronger elastic!' On *Calling All Forces* the next week it was Googie Withers as a Hollywood movie star graduating from cheap two-reelers to feature film stardom who found herself feeding Ted Ray with the line, 'I finally walked out of those crummy shorts!' Every pretty girl from Diana Dors ('I've got a lot of bare-faced cheek, haven't I?') to a fledgling Marilyn Monroe in Britain on a Bob Hope troop show gave Ted the cue for his celebrated reply.

After two years of varying the feedlines with tireless but sometimes dogged invention, Monkhouse and Goodwin dropped the gag. Bob Monkhouse at Kempton Park seven years later heard it as an automatic answer to the cry, 'They're off!' Ted Ray kept it in his stage act for several years, pretending to find a frilly pair of panties on the stage after a female performer had made her exit. As he eyed the knickers, some wit in the audience usually beat him to it - 'She should have used stronger elastic, Ted!' 'So should your mother,' Ted would fire back. 'Then you wouldn't be here!'

you silly little man! Richard Murdoch to Arthur Askey in *Band Waggon*.
Murdoch: (instructing Arthur how to court Nausea Bagwash, with whom he was supposed to be in love) You say, 'Darling Nausea, your lips are like petals . . .'
Askey: Nausea, darling, your lips are like

petals - bicycle petals.
Murdoch: No, no, no. You silly little man.

you silly twisted boy! Usually said to
Neddie Seagoon, *The Goon Show.*

you've got a big red conk! *Ray's A Laugh.*